Stenciling
MADE EASY

JOANNA SHEEN

CRESCENT BOOKS
NEW YORK • AVENEL, NEW JERSEY

This 1995 edition published by Crescent Books,
a division of Random House Value Publishing, Inc.
40 Engelhard Avenue, Avenel, New Jersey 07001.

Random House
New York • Toronto • London • Sydney • Auckland

ISBN: 0-517-14293-7

Produced by Haldane Mason, London

Acknowledgements:
Art Direction: Ron Samuels
Editor: Lisa Dyer
Design: Paul Cooper
Photography: Joff Lee
Styling: John Lee Studios

Contents

Introduction

Stenciling is an art form that can be handled by the youngest or least-skilled member of a family with great success. The very professional results that can be achieved with stencils belie the simplicity behind the technique; once you have mastered the first few simple strokes, it is plain sailing nearly all the way!

It is very unusual for any form of artistic decoration to result in near-perfect results from the very beginning, but it can be so with stenciling. The most difficult process is designing and cutting stencils. This being so, you may prefer to purchase ready-cut stencils from the extensive collections available, and you will be certain to achieve wonderful results on your first project.

Once you progress to creating your own stencils, you will find inspiration all around you. A color magazine accompanying the Sunday paper can provide great ideas for designs just as easily as a trip to an historic house or museum. Often a sheet of wrapping paper, wallpaper, or even an advertisement in a magazine can be as inspirational as more complicated and beautiful images. Look for simple shapes that work well, and experiment on lining paper or other scrap paper before you begin.

You will find many different ideas in this book. There are projects to show you how to stencil on a range of different surfaces, from terracotta and wood to fabric, paper, and walls. Once you feel confident with the stenciling techniques, then many other ideas will occur to you and stenciling will become a very useful and enjoyable craft skill to have and use.

The list of possible projects for stenciling is endless, as I am sure you will find once you have started. You can create beautiful decorations for your home, or you can decorate or create your own greeting cards or wrapping paper, thereby adding your own personal touch and saving money too. Look for objects to decorate at flea markets and rummage sales. Furniture that appears to need some repair often needs only a good clean, a coat of paint, and some fun with a stencil effect to create a beautiful piece of furniture that will be much admired. Read the basic techniques section (see pages 16–17) carefully before you start a project. Make sure you are happy with the basic ideas, never apply too much paint at once, always add a little more if it is too faint, take care and work slowly but surely, and you have a lot of fun ahead of you.

One word of warning! Once you have mastered the art of stenciling, then stenciling anything and everything soon becomes the order of the day! A successfully stenciled bedroom soon leads to the living room, kitchen, and garage all being decorated with huge enthusiasm. Do remember it *is* possible to have a room left in the house that is not stenciled (I haven't!) when the urge to stencil comes upon you. I am sure you will have a lot of fun and satisfaction from this craft with a minimum amount of effort and investment.

A Brief History of Stenciling

Stenciling has been a popular craft and simple form of printing for centuries, and the skill dates back as early as the second century AD. Japan and China have very fine stenciling traditions, and many early examples exist of each country's art.

Chinese stenciling dates from about 600 AD, when pieces of leather, wood, or vellum were used as the stencil rather than paper. Images were stenciled on cave walls, pieces of silk, and leather armor. The image of a sitting Buddha is a popular one with early Chinese stenciling – and, indeed, it does make a good, simple motif if your project needs that theme in the design.

Japanese stenciling developed to decorate silk and fabrics for clothing and decorative purposes. The decoration on the garments would vary with the importance and social standing of the wearer, and a Samurai warrior's silk kimono would have much more elaborate and gilded decoration than a simple worker's costume, which may have had only a simple indigo stencil on cotton fabric. The Japanese refined their stenciling skills and continued to develop and improve their craft

long after similar traditions in other countries were being overtaken by the Industrial Revolution and the development of machine-printing.

Japanese stencils were not manufactured from wood or leather like the Chinese versions, but were made from a paper-like substance formed from the bark of a mulberry tree. The paper was made more supple by soaking it for some time in the juice of persimmons, a process which made the stencil waterproof and able to withstand more wear and tear. Because the Japanese had developed their skills to such impressively high levels, their complex stencils were very different to the simpler designs used in other cultures. Their bridges, or ties, to hold the stencil together, were far less obvious and, in many cases, were non-existent. Where we would expect to have a good solid ⅛ in (3 mm) of rigid card, they might have a few gossamer-thin silk threads or a fine mesh of silken threads, which gave their work even more detail and made the bridges virtually invisible once the design was printed. Today, Japan still has a fine stenciling movement with many wonderful books on the subject being published, and a good selection of paints and tools available.

European stenciling has its origin in Rome, where it was used as a rudimentary printing process in the second century AD. Later, the process became popular throughout many areas of Europe, including France and England. The materials needed to produce a stencil, and the paints required, were expensive and scarce, so most of the work was commissioned by people and institutions who could afford this form of decoration. As a result, early stenciling appears mostly on large buildings, such as mansions, churches, and cathedrals. Simple repeat patterns were used to decorate walls, and more complex floral or animal designs were used to decorate paper and fabric.

Stenciled designs, either on paper or painted straight onto distempered walls, were a much cheaper method of reproducing the decorative fabric and tapestry that traditionally hung on walls. Hand-stenciled wallpaper would have been less than a quarter of the price of damask or cut velvet at the time. However, this popularity and economy led, in some ways, to the demise of hand-stenciled paper. As stenciling became more and more popular, so printing methods were developed to supersede the hand-finished versions and make decorative wallpaper even less expensive.

Gradually stenciling became used by all classes in society, and the decoration would appear in a relatively humble worker's cottage as well as in a beautiful palace. Stenciling also came back into vogue with the Art Nouveau movement at the end of the nineteenth century. In Britain, there is evidence that William Morris used stencils for wallpaper and ceilings, and many architects of the time, especially William Burges and, later, Charles Rennie Mackintosh, used stencils to great effect on furniture and interiors. Wonderful examples of British stenciling design can be found in museums, stately homes, churches, and other historical buildings throughout Great Britian.

A very strong tradition and history of stenciling also exists in America. Although wallpapers were imported from Europe and later manufactured in America, the cost was prohibitively high and beyond the means of the majority of the early settlers. Stenciling became enormously popular, and decorated walls, floors, fabric, and furniture. There are some wonderful designs dating from the nineteenth century, including repeat wall designs and also large single motifs using fruit, flowers, and birds. These natural images of plants and animals were exceedingly popular in American decorative arts.

The colors used in early American stenciling are cruder than the more refined European pigments. Natural pigments were mixed into a paste with whey from the household milk supply. They had a mellow richness that was very different to the exotic colors being used in Europe at the time. Although many householders enjoyed stenciling their homes and fabrics, most of the work seems to have been done by a traveling band of craftsmen who would wander from town to town, offering their skills to the settlers and decorating walls or chairs, cupboards or chests, as required.

Much has been written about American patchwork quilts, but bedspreads were also decorated with beautiful stencil work. Stenciled decoration was also commonly used on furniture – mainly as an attempt to copy fine lacquer designs from the East. However, in my opinion, the finished results often surpass that which they were intended to copy. There are beautiful chests and cupboards, chairs and tables from the early American period, all finely decorated and many still quite exquisite. A good representation of these stenciled objects can be seen at national and local museums throughout the country. They show that stenciling, despite being a craft all of us can enjoy, can produce special pieces that are truly remarkable when a really talented craftsperson executes the work.

Tools and Materials

One of the greatest bonuses of stenciling as a decorating medium is the moderate cost of materials needed to totally transform a room. In fact, once that initial investment is made, the cost would probably cover transforming an entire house, not just one room or object. The basic equipment you will need are brushes, or other applicators for applying the color, stencils, paints, and a pencil and ruler for planning the position of your design. If you intend to make your own stencils, you will need additional materials, depending on the method you choose, as described below. Most of the tools and materials you will need are available from art and craft suppliers, from special stenciling and home-decorating stores, or in the craft section in department stores. Some specialist equipment is available from mail-order companies. Look in your phone book for specialist companies who will be able to help you find unusual items.

Brushes and other applicators

Some type of applicator will be necessary for applying the color, and this will depend on your budget as well as your preferred method of working. Experimenting with various applicators before you start a project will help you decide which type works best for you.

It is essential to have a different applicator for each color included in a project. So, if you are planning a three- or four-color design, then three or four brushes will be needed.

Synthetic sponges make the least expensive applicators, but using them is not easier – just less expensive. Natural sponges can also be used, provided they have small holes. A sponge can be cut into several pieces, and each piece used for a different color.

Sponge applicators are special stenciling tools. They are very easy to control, allowing you to fill in tiny, detailed areas of the stencil.

Commercial stenciling brushes are stubby brushes with short, stiff bristles. They make stenciling much easier and will give good professional results with the minimum of fuss and effort. The size of brush you will need depends on the scale of your project. If you are using a large, relatively undetailed stencil and are decorating a wall or floor, then a larger size of brush, such as a size 6, is quicker and easier to handle. If you are tackling a smaller project or using more detailed stencils, then a more moderate size 4 brush is better. A size 2 brush is ideal if you are trying to capture some small details or using an intricate stencil.

Cleaning brushes and applicators

If you are using oil-based paints, some brush cleaner, mineral spirit or turpentine will be needed for cleaning. If you are using fabric paints or latex paint, then warm water will clean the brushes adequately. Always read the instructions on the paint carefully, so brushes or other applicators can be cleaned correctly in order to prolong their life.

Scissors

8

Stencil-making equipment

As a beginner, it is far easier to buy plastic or card ready-made stencils (see page 14). But should you find that your enthusiasm leads you to making your own stencils, then another outlay of equipment becomes necessary.

There are two basic methods for making stencils. The first method (see page 12) is more difficult, but less expensive, and you will need a scalpel or craft knife, a cutting board or mat to protect surfaces, pencils and pens, tracing paper, and stencil card or paper. The second method (see pages 12–13) is a little more costly, but much easier to do well, and you will need an electric stencil cutter, a sheet of glass, and some opaque stencil plastic.

Stencil card or paper is a specially treated paper produced by soaking manila paper in linseed oil, which makes it tough, waterproof, and more like cardboard.

Stencil plastic is a transparent plastic sold in different thicknesses. A middle-range is best to use: if the plastic is too thick, it is difficult to cut, and if too thin, it will bend too much.

Electric stencil cutters are available, at a moderate cost, by mail-order or from some craft or home-decorating stores. The stencil cutter cuts through sheets of stencil plastic like a knife through butter, and fluid curves are immediately a success because you "trace" your design with the cutter.

Other useful supplies

Along with such items as paper towels and cloths to clean spills and protect surfaces, you will find it useful to have masking tape, a ruler, pencils, felt-tip pens, a wax pencil, tracing paper, and graph paper. A large sheet of glass is not only necessary for cutting stencils with a stencil cutter, but it makes a useful palette for paints. You could also use an old plate or saucer, or small bowls or plastic containers.

Masking tape

Electric stencil cutter

Scalpel

Ruler

Glass sheet

Size 2 stenciling brush

Size 6 stenciling brush

Size 4 stenciling brush

Cotton swabs

Natural sponge

Synthetic sponge

Eraser

Paints

The type of paint you need depends heavily on the surface you are going to tackle (see page 11).

Latex paints can be used on many surfaces, but you will need to make a real effort at keeping the paint as dry as possible. You can buy small cans or sample pots of latex colors to use, and these are available in a vast range of colors.

Oil-based stenciling crayons are a moderate investment initially, but are extremely long-lasting and have a wide range of applications. These crayons, or paint sticks, are excellent for use on all flat-finished walls, whether lined or wood-chip finish, and are versatile enough to use on other flat surfaces, such as terra-cotta, painted or stained wood, and even fabric if you are not concerned about a long-term washable finish. With these paints, subtle variations in color are simple to achieve using light or variable pressure. A wide selection of colors is available.

Fabric paints are essential for decorating any fabric project where you would like to be able to wash the finished item. The paints are available in a smaller range of colors than the stenciling crayons, and it is not easy to create lighter or darker shades just by using variations of pressure when applying the color. However, the paints are still very enjoyable to use and widen the field of household items you can decorate considerably. The designs will not, however, last indefinitely, and limited washing is probably the best option.

Water-based ink pads are simple to use and perfect for paper-based projects. They are excellent because the ink pads are very dry and the range of colors is wide.

Aerosol spray paints produce some of the most beautiful stencil effects, but they do take some time and practice to perfect. It is all too easy to overspray an area, or to accidentally spray a part of the design that should have been covered. Masking off areas outside the stencil may be necessary, because spray paints tend to spread. Also, be sure to work in a well-ventilated area.

Other paints are also available, and you could use acrylics, watercolors, gouache, or metallic paints, or any other form of color

Water-based ink pads

Oil-based stenciling crayons

Fabric paints

Choosing and using color

You do not initially need a large palette of colors to begin stenciling. You might like to choose the exact colors you need for your first project, and then gradually build up a collection, or else start with a reasonable range of useful basic colors. When choosing the color scheme for your project, think carefully about the base or background color. Paler colors are effective on a pale cream or white wall, while a dark wooden background will need a much stronger color for the design to register. Terra-cotta will soak up color and needs strong amounts of very pale or strong color for the design to show up well.

Latex paint tends to look similar in the container to the finished effect on the wall. This is not the case with the oil-based stenciling crayons. In many cases, these look almost black in the stick, but may be a strong blue, green or purple when applied. A dark blue can be applied very lightly to give a paler blue effect.

Gold and silver are available in fabric paints, oil-based paints, and powders. A touch of gold always adds glamor, and all the metallic shades look attractive on their own or mixed with basic colors.

Although you can mix colors on a glass palette (like the one used throughout this book), using a single color is much easier. Paints can also be mixed directly on the design (see page 17). All paints can dry out quickly. If you buy small cans of paints, then simply replace the lid. With paint crayons, use a resealable plastic bag for each stick of color.

Preparing surfaces

If you are uncertain how your paint will react to a specific surface, it is a good idea to paint a small sample on an inconspicuous area first. All surfaces should be clean, dry, and dust- and grease-free.

Surfaces painted with a flat latex paint are the best for most stenciling projects. Even a textured wallpaper can be stenciled on if it has been painted with a flat latex paint. Avoid gloss finishes because the paint will not absorb. A painted surface that is peeling, whether plaster or wood, will need to be stripped down or sanded and repainted, to provide a smooth, clean surface. If you are stenciling on a fabric, you will need to make sure the fabric is preshrunk and colorfast. Natural fabrics are best to use, and avoid any glazed fabrics.

RIGHT From the top: natural wood surface, heavy paper or cardboard surface, heavy muslin fabric, terra-cotta tile.

that appeals to you. Ceramic paints can be used for decorating plates and tiles, but because they will not have the durability of kiln-fired ceramic, care should be taken with how you use and where you place the decorated object.

Varnishes

Your color must be set carefully with a varnish so the design will not wear off. Use an artist's fixative, aerosol spray varnish, or paint a coat of varnish on top of your design. Sealing with varnish is especially important for walls in areas of heavy traffic, or if you are decorating the seat of a chair, or a surface that will receive a lot of wear and tear.

Cutting Out a Stencil

There are two methods that can be used to produce a stencil: the first uses stencil card and a craft knife or scalpel, and the second uses an electric stencil cutter with stencil plastic. Both methods are possible, but the second is a lot less work than the other. Cutting through the card stencil with a scalpel can be hard work, because cutting curves with a straight blade is not always as easy as it looks. Both methods are described here, though, because you may wish to use both at some time or another. Refer to page 9 for the materials you will need. Both begin with an original pattern or template to trace, such as those available from craft magazines or books.

Using the opaque plastic for projects, as opposed to the buff stencil card, is another major benefit. If you are using a stencil cut from card, you cannot see the background onto which you are stenciling – if you are stenciling a border of a repetitive design, then being able to see what you have already stenciled, or where the edges of the wall are positioned, makes life easier!

Enlarging and reducing

If the design that inspires you is a little too large or too small, then it can be increased or decreased in size by photocopying the template.

Alternatively, you can size your picture up or down by using squared graph paper, and this method is perfect for enlarging or reducing the size of templates, patterns, or simple line drawings (for more on sourcing templates, see page 15). To enlarge or reduce the size of a template, place a sheet of gridded tracing paper over the picture and trace the design.

LEFT Place a suitably large piece of glass over your template. Tape the stencil plastic onto the glass, or just hold it down with your free hand.

Then copy the design, square by square, onto a larger grid for an enlarged size or a smaller grid for a smaller size.

Cutting a stencil from card

First you need to trace your design from the original template to the stenciling card. To trace the design, copy the template onto tracing paper with a pencil. Turn the traced design over, place on top of the card, and retrace to transfer the design to the card (the reverse side of the card will be the right side up). You could also use a sheet of carbon paper inserted between the tracing paper and the card to transfer the design.

It is important to remember to leave a wide margin all around the design, of at least 3 in (7.5 cm), so when you apply the color you will not brush paint onto other areas.

When your design is traced on the card, go over the design once again with a strong, black felt-tip pen, so it is clear and simple to cut out. You may find it easier to black out each piece to be cut out.

Work on a table with plenty of space, so you can swivel your piece of card in all directions rather than moving your body. Protect your table with a rubberized cutting mat, thick cardboard, or thin wood. Always cut out the more delicate pieces of the design first, before tackling the large sweeps and curves.

Cutting a stencil from plastic

This method is far easier, and no cutting mat is required because sharp tools will not be near the table. However, great care must be taken that the electric stencil cutter is switched on only when it is needed.

LEFT A wax pencil can be used to trace the design onto the clear plastic before you cut it, but you may find it easier just to cut directly onto the plastic without following this step.

Begin by tracing the template, enlarging or reducing the image if necessary. Cut a piece of plastic the correct size for the design – remembering to leave a good 3 in (7.5 cm) border all around the design. Place a sheet of glass over your traced template, then cover the glass with the stencil plastic. Tape the plastic to the glass with masking tape, if necessary. I generally just hold the plastic in position with my left hand while using the cutter in my right. If you feel nervous about cutting directly onto the plastic, you can trace the design first with a wax pencil.

Allow the stencil cutter to warm up for about 5 minutes. With an easy, even pressure, "trace" over the stencil design with the stencil cutter, as though it were a pencil or felt-tip pen. Do not stay in one spot for too long, or the cutter will melt an irregular patch from the plastic.

Once you have completed the cutting, place the stencil cutter in a safe place. With a gentle but sure movement, pull the stencil plastic away from the piece of glass. Where the stencil cutter has melted the plastic onto the glass, the plastic will adhere to the glass, leaving you a clean stencil to use. If this does not happen, then gently push through any loose pieces.

If you make a mistake when you are cutting the stencil by either method, then you can remedy the problem with a piece of masking tape. Use a very small scrap on both the front and back of the stencil.

Cutting a multiple stencil

Often a design is simple enough to cut as just one stencil, but in other cases you may find it necessary to split the design into its various color components. The main benefit from this is that you only need to paint one color per stencil, rather than trying to maneuver around smaller details, remembering separate colors. If you want to split a stencil into separate colors, then just trace around the elements of the design

ABOVE When you have finished cutting the design, gently but firmly pull the sheet away from the glass. Press out all the loose pieces that have not been left behind on the glass sheet, and your stencil is ready to use.

that need the first color for your first stencil, and then do the same with separate stencil card or plastic for the second color, and so on. Number and color-code each stencil. Cutting small notches in two opposite corners through all the stencils will help you to line up the individual components to make the overall design. You can then pencil around the notches once the stencil is in position on the object, and use the pencil marks to register the next stencil.

RIGHT Allow approximately five minutes for the stencil cutter to reach the correct temperature. Using an even but moderate amount of pressure, "trace" the design with the sharp tip of the cutter pressing into the plastic.

Using Ready-made Stencils

Precut commercial stencils are available from a wide selection of outlets. Arts and crafts suppliers usually sell a diverse range, as do special home-decorating stores. Women's magazines often include features on stenciling, including actual stencils or templates to trace. However, the best source of ready-cut stencils is from one of the many mail-order companies (see suppliers on pages 100–101), who offer a dazzling array of designs to give you inspiration and ideas for adding stenciling details to every conceivable place in the home. These ready-cut stencils have been designed by experienced stenciling professionals who have solved any problems with that particular design, and this makes them much easier for a beginner to use.

If you start your stenciling by using a commercial stencil, you have a very high chance of producing a splendid finished result first time around. Progressing to designing and cutting your own stencils is best done after you have become proficient at the actual paint and finishing techniques.

Professional stencils are nearly always sold on clear or opaque plastic for the same reasons that I recommend using clear plastic to cut your own stencils: the plastic allows you to see the work you have just completed and to keep to a continual line of work ahead of you.

Card stencils, such as the ones at the back of this book, are not as long-lasting as their more rigid plastic counterparts, but work perfectly well.

Ready-cut stencils can be taken at face value and used in exactly the way they were designed. It is also useful to consider separate pieces of the stencil. By masking off some of the details, you may be able to use just a ribbon or bow on its own, or pick out a single flower to repeat as a random motif. Some stencils are accompanied by ideas for different uses, and these can mean very good value because many different projects can be completed with only a few stencils. But equally good value can be obtained by purchasing your designs carefully and reusing various parts of the stencil.

LEFT Good, precut stencils are an excellent investment, because they are long-wearing and designed by professionals. They are available in a huge range of designs.

Storing and cleaning stencils

If you have collected quite a few stencils, then keep them stored way as cleanly and carefully as you can. An easy and efficient way to file them is to use large envelopes or folders, and to stencil a one-color version of the design onto the front of each so you can see at a glance which stencil is inside.

Stencils must be cleaned immediately after you have finished with them. If you are using the oil-based crayons, then a piece of clean paper towel is usually sufficient. If you are using latex or a similar water-soluble paint, then wash the stencil (if it is plastic) before storing it away.

BELOW To adapt ready-made stencils to your own designs, choose the section of the stencil you want to keep and mask off all other areas of your stencil with strips of masking tape on both sides.

Creating Your Own Stencils

Although there is a plethora of ready-made designs and stencils available in the marketplace, there may be several reasons why you prefer to create your own designs. Obviously, there is the cost element, as it is much less expensive to produce your own stencils than to buy someone else's ideas, but also there may be a more aesthetic reason. Perhaps you have always desired a flight of hot-air balloons ascending into the spare bedroom ceiling, or a flock of sheep galloping across the nursery walls, and simply can not find a suitable stencil pattern in any of the commercial catalogs. Creating your own design is then the answer.

Inspirations and ideas can be gleaned from many places: newspaper color supplements,

ABOVE A simple car motif for a boy's bedroom is found in an advertisement. Place the glass sheet over the car photograph.

magazines and papers, books, textile designs, and advertisements, to name but a few. Any picture or design you find can simply be traced at the same size. If the design that inspires you is a little too large or too small, then it can be increased or decreased in size by photocopying, or you can resize your picture using graph paper (see page 12). Tracing actual objects can be one of the easiest ways to find suitable designs for your stencils. For example, pressed leaves can be drawn around or traced to help you create a leafy autumnal effect, or doilies can be used as stencils to give a pretty, lacy design.

If you have an attractive curtain, you could trace a small part of the fabric design to create a coordinating border or random design on the

ABOVE Cover the glass with a suitable piece of stencil plastic and, using an electric stencil cutter, trace around the shape of the car. Remember to include bridges to hold the stencil together.

walls. Children's books are also a great source for nursery ideas.

You must remember that for a stencil design to work, there must be legs or bridges to support the stencil. The bridges should be at least ⅛ in (3 mm) wide.

Examine your design and look for suitable places to insert the bridges. If the bridges of your stencil become too weak, false supports can be put in with neat strips of masking tape. All stencil designs need to be bold and flowing; practice is definitely the name of the game. Once your pattern is traced, follow the instructions for cutting a stencil from card or plastic on pages 12 and 13.

Basic Techniques

Stenciling is merely a method of directing where the paint is applied, and the way you use your stencil can be as varied as the patterns and colors of your projects. The very first step with all sten- ciling projects is to prepare the surface of the item you want to decorate (see page 11) and make sure all the materials you will need are easily at hand (see pages 8–11).

Planning your design
If you are creating a continuous border or repeated pattern in a line, it is a good idea to draw a thin pencil line along the base of where the stencil will rest. The pencil marks can be erased later, and the line will help keep the design straight and even. A random pattern usually only needs a good eye and constant checks that the designs are evenly spaced out. You may like to trace the entire design lightly onto the surface, especially if you are working with fabrics and other materials where there is no chance for correcting mistakes, or where exact spacing is required.

ABOVE To position a stencil on a curved surface, tape the stencil in place with masking tape. You will need to use a reasonable amount of pressure to hold the stencil flat while you are applying paint.

Positioning your stencil
You may want to attach your stencil to the wall or surface you are decorating – although, in some cases, it is just as easy to hold the stencil with your free hand. Attach the stencil with several small pieces of masking tape. This tape is fairly good-natured and, if removed carefully, does not take paint off a wall or surface. Another alternative is to spray some spray adhesive onto the back of the stencil; the adhesive will make the stencil tacky and you will be able to reposition it five or six times. Personally, I find spray adhesive sticky and messy, and it has once damaged the paintwork on a wall I was decorating. If you do use the adhesive, test it first on an inconspicuous area of the wall or object you are decorating.

Applying the color
Once you are happy with your method of securing the stencil, you are ready to apply the paint. Make sure all your colors are easily available, preferably on a glass palette. The most popular applicator is the stenciling brush. The brush is used in an upright manner, and the paint gently applied with a slightly circular movement. You could choose to use a stippling method with the brush, or work around the edges first with a circular movement leaving the center areas white. If you use a sponge, the paint can be dabbed on in short punchy movements to achieve a slightly patchy effect, which looks wonderfully rustic and antique.

ABOVE If you want your stencil design to be centered, first find the center of your object. If you are working on a flat, square object, make sure all the angles are right angles and measure and mark an exact center point on all four sides. Lightly mark a pencil line from top to bottom and side to side to connect the points. You can then position your stencil over the cross.

Dab any excess paint off the brush or sponge first, and apply the paint as drily as possible, starting with the lightest color first. The paint is best applied lightly, and if you wish to strengthen the color, another coat can be applied to the same area. Repeating an application of paint to enhance the color is far preferable to putting the paint on too thickly in the first place. After you have applied the first color, remove the stencil and check the density of color. If you are not happy with the result, replace the stencil and gently add a little more paint.

Allow the first color to dry completely before repeating with the remaining series of colors, and check the back of your stencil occasionally to make sure it is clean.

Many of the media you choose to use can be mixed by painting one color over another. A dark center in the middle of a flower can be created by using the lighter color first, and then adding the darker color later. Always apply the lighter color first; this way you will get two clearly defined shades. If you try to apply the darker paint first, the two shades blend and are indistinguishable.

Finishing your design

After the last coat of paint is dry, set your design by using an artist's fixative or varnish (see page 11). For hardwearing surfaces, you may need to apply several coats of varnish. If you are in any doubt as to which sealant or varnish is best for the paints you are using and the object you are stenciling, read the manufacturer's recommendations included with the paints. With fabric

paints, follow the manufacturer's instructions included; usually pressing the fabric is the correct way to set the colors.

Random pattern
Here a simple duck stencil has been applied at random, without any preconceived ideas of placement. A random composition eliminates the need for measuring.

Ordered pattern
Here the duck motif has been used in a formal, ordered composition. All small motifs can be used in a variety of ways to make stripes, borders, diagonals, and squares. Some planning is usually needed because it is essential not to run out of space before you have completed a full design.

Stippling
A stippled paint effect is achieved by loading a stenciling brush fairly heavily with paint and holding it upright, then dabbing onto the stencil until the area to be covered is completely painted.

Sponged effect
This sponged paint effect is produced using a small, dry natural sponge with oil-based stenciling crayons. The sponge is rubbed into the paint and then dabbed over the area to be stenciled, and an airy, textured finish is the result. The center of the flower has been sponged a second time with some brown to add a little shading.

Circular-motion stencil brush
This flower has been painted using a size 4 standard stenciling brush. The brush is moved in a circular motion, which gives depth and intensity to the color, and can produce lighter or heavier shading.

Edging
Here an edging effect is achieved by using a standard stenciling brush and a minimal amount of paint. The brush is moved in a circular motion, but only around the edge of the flower, and then a tiny amount of coverage in the middle. This effect is easier to achieve on a larger image, and looks especially striking when the background color is strong.

Projects

These projects are simple to do and stunning in effect. Just follow
the steps, and you will find it easy to transform an ugly old chest
into a magical children's toy-box, or bare white walls into a
beautiful arbor of roses. All the ideas are designed to
inspire you to try creating your own stencils,
designs, and color combinations, as
well as helping you to practice
the basic skills of stenciling.

Teddy Bear Time

Painting Charming Designs on Nursery Walls

One of the many good points about stenciling is the moderate cost involved. When a new baby is imminent, and there are so many other demands on the budget, a stenciled design in the nursery can achieve a lovely effect with minimal expense. When planning your stencil for a nursery or small child's room, keep the design simple and uncluttered. The choice of color is obviously a personal one, but often primary colors are more popular with children. A soft, dreamy color scheme that you find irresistible may be rejected by a "discerning" two-year-old who would much prefer a design in bright fire-engine red, with a touch of emerald green and banana yellow thrown in for good measure!

If you want to create your own designs for children's walls, there are many interesting and attractive ideas suitable for children. You could plan your design around a favorite cartoon or storybook character, or use a general theme, such as transportation, the circus, or farm animals. The fabrics you have chosen for the room often provide good inspiration for a stencil design, and an image can be traced from curtains or bed linen. With a new baby you obviously have a free hand, so whatever theme delights you is a possibility. Hot-air balloons fading into the distance, fluffy lambs, alphabet letters, or tractors all make charming designs.

There are many precut stencils available that are specially designed for children, and these would be ideal if you do not feel comfortable with cutting out stencils. You could also combine one of your own designs with a ready-made stencil, by adding a balloon motif to a precut teddy bear stencil, for example.

Plan your decorating scheme carefully before you start work. First of all, decide on a random pattern, an ordered composition, or a combination of the two. One possibility would involve a carefully measured border of regimented toy soldiers at the height of a picture rail, or as a divider between two colors or types of wallpaper. Another idea would be to use a border design at one height, with a random design making a wallpaper effect above or beneath the border.

When you have decided on your decoration and have prepared your surface (see page 11), lightly mark the walls with crosses or lines in pencil, so you obtain the effect you want with the correct spacing or randomness. It will be too late to correct the design after you have stenciled it in the wrong position!

Materials

- Teddy bear and duck stencils (see Stencil Templates, page 103)
- Masking tape
- Oil-based stenciling crayons in red, orange and blue, or colors of your choice
- Size 4 stenciling brushes
- Glass palette
- Satin or flat aerosol spray varnish

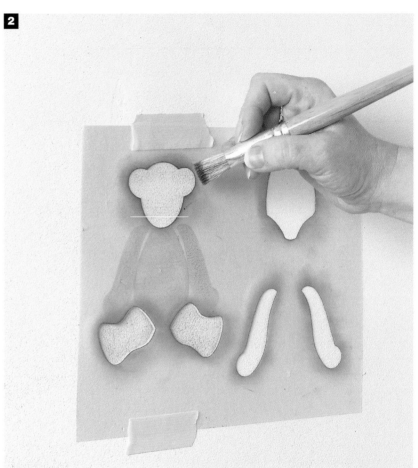

1 Before you start, make sure your walls are clean, dry, and painted with a flat latex paint. Make sure you have an applicator for each color. You will not need to plan your design, because this is a randomly spaced pattern.

2 Begin with the teddy bears' bodies, arms, and legs, and apply the first color lightly, painting another coat to darken, if necessary. Paint the bears randomly around the room, leaving enough space to add the ducks and bricks.

3 Add a contrasting color for the bear's paws and bow, such as the blue used here, taking care to position the stencil accurately so the bow is in the correct place and does not cover the bear's face. Add the paws and bows.

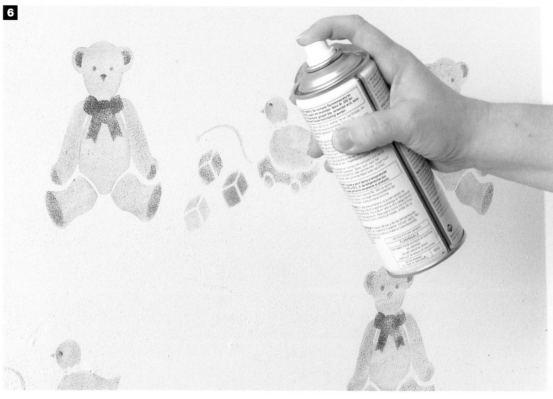

4 Next add the stencil design for the duck on wheels and bricks. Use several colors on this stencil, with one color for the duck and two or three more for the bricks and wagon. Accuracy is important, and you may prefer to use a size 2 stenciling brush rather than a size 4 brush.

5 Using a cotton swab, rub the end into a little of the blue paint, or another color if you prefer. Gently dab the cotton swab in the correct position on the duck to create an eye. Repeat for all the eyes.

BELOW So many different colorways are possible for this design, from pastels to vivid hues. Bright colors may be more appealing for young children, but you must also take into account the overall color scheme of the room and the fact that, with luck, your work will last for many years.

6 Once you are happy with the finished paintwork and the entire project has been completed, spray the design with varnish. Choose satin or flat varnish, because gloss varnish is too heavy for a latex paint base.

OPPOSITE This charming design adds a delicate softness to a nursery wall, and is suitable for either a boy's or girl's room.

Wild Roses

Using Trailing Patterns on Bedroom Walls

There are many shapes and sizes to use in stencil decoration, and the rose design chosen here illustrates a free-form pattern that can be adapted as you progress. Some thought is needed beforehand to plan the spread and location of your design, but exact measurements are not necessary. If you feel really unsure about committing a stenciled rose to the wall without prior sketching or planning, then you could stencil a few of the large roses onto lining paper and lightly tape them in position to give you a rough idea of the number and general size of the decoration you want. Although this rose design has been suggested as a bedroom decoration, any wall can be decorated in this manner. The roses could make just as attractive a scheme in a hallway or main living area, as in a bedroom.

When you are using a solid, geometrical pattern or a straight repeat design, it becomes crucial that you get the measuring and repeat spacing perfect, or the images that are just a little too far apart will catch your eye forever! However, with most floral designs you can easily add a twig, tendril, spray of leaves, or a few buds – whatever blends with the overall design – to extend or fill in a basic composition. This is particularly useful should you feel there is an empty

patch you would like to fill, or a design you would like to twist around a corner. A lovely flowing bough of willow or sprays of spring catkins are so easy to add to and twist by adding an extra branch here and there!

There are many different textures and surfaces of walls that can be stenciled, depending on the type of paint you use (see page 10). If you are using the oil-based stencil crayons, as shown here, then make sure the surface is painted with a flat rather than a gloss paint, or that your wallpaper is flat and does not have a glossy finish.

A wall painted with a pale color is usually the easiest and most successful for stenciling. Bright colors and vivid patterns show up well against a pale background, as do soft pastels; this certainly makes a light background the most versatile. If you find white too stark, try a magnolia or buttermilk color to add warmth. A dark background can be very effective when stenciled with gold or silver paint, such as in a night sky scheme with stars and moons, or gold fleur-de-lis against a bottle-green background. White and other very light colors also show up moderately well on dark backgrounds, but I would still advise caution because dark colors are more difficult to paint over.

Materials
- Rose stencils
- Oil-based stenciling crayons in reds and greens, or colors of your choice
- Size 2, 4 and 6 stenciling brushes
- Glass palette
- Satin or flat aerosol spray varnish

1 Before starting, make sure your walls are prepared and you have a brush for each color you will use. This design is intended to be halfway between a random design and a carefully placed frieze. The roses tumble down the wall and can be added into the design freehand.

2 Paint the leaves first to establish the size and range of the design, leaving space for the flowers.

3 Add some roses into the design, using a pale red and concentrating on the outer part of the flower. The darker middle will be added later. All the roses can be the same color, or you could mix various shades.

4 Using a darker red, shade in the center of the flower and shade some of the edges of the petals to give extra interest to the design and some variation in the overall color.

5 Add extra leaves to pad out the design where you feel there is too large a gap. Leaves are always useful fillers because they are unstructured, particularly in this type of design, and they can always be used to add a little extra color here and there.

6 Once you have finished the design and are happy with it, spray the design with varnish. This will help give the paintwork a longer life and help it resist knocks and scratches.

OPPOSITE Trailing roses look beautiful in rooms. You may like to continue the effect down to the floor at the corners of the room.

Helpful Tips

● A size 6 stenciling brush is essential for larger designs on walls, like the roses here. If you try to use a smaller brush, you will get a very patchy effect. Large brushes are also useful for stenciling floors.

LEFT When you are considering which color scheme to use, it is not necessary to stick rigidly to natural or lifelike colors. Here, the roses have been colored blue, and the effect is just as attractive. Exploring unconventional possibilities makes the number of choices limitless.

BELOW When you are redecorating a room with a new theme, such as these roses, the idea can be carried through with complementary stencils to decorate other parts of the room, like drawers or curtain tie-backs.

BELOW You can use a stencil like this one for a trailing project, combined with various other components from other stencils, each used singly. Alternatively, you can make or buy a stencil with more detail on each piece, so only one or two stencils need to be used.

Iris by the Stream

Stenciling on Bathroom Walls and Tiles

Bathrooms can be ideal candidates for stencil effects, because they are usually fairly small rooms and there will be less area to stencil than with a large living space. Most people spend a limited amount of time in the bathroom, so it is fun to create a really striking design that has a lot of impact when you enter the room. Elaborate or overpowering designs are not well suited for large rooms in which you are going to spend much greater amounts of time because you may tire of the effect very quickly!

I have always felt the need to decorate bathrooms with a vaguely watery theme, such as water lilies, shells, ponds, or seaside or river bank scenes. This is not necessary, though, and no doubt there are many designs that would look stunning in your bathroom that do not have even a remote connection with anything vaguely wet or watery.

A design on the ceiling of a bathroom can be very effective. However, I can not recommend an easy way to apply the paint – it is definitely a two-person job, or, alternatively, use the same method as Michelangelo with the Sistine Chapel and lie on scaffolding!

Walls covered with ceramic tiles can also be decorated with small random designs, or even one large design. Use ceramic paints for

decorating tiles, but do not expect the painted tiles to have the same hardwearing nature as fired tiles. So, if your bathroom is heavily used, and particularly if you have young children who may inadvertently scratch the tiles, then you may have to retouch or paint over the design when deterioration sets in. A special ceramic sealant is useful to varnish the tiles after decorating, but you could also use a standard varnish.

You may also like to stencil bathroom accessories to match your overall theme. For example, a shell motif used on the walls could be repeated on a mirror frame, laundry basket, or cupboards, perhaps in another size. Alternatively, look to your existing bathroom decor. For example, if you have old-fashioned colored tiles on the floor, repeat those colors in a striking geometric pattern used as a wall border or on a mirror frame.

As with all surfaces to be stenciled with oil-based crayons, the walls must be clean, grease-free, and completely dry before you start work. The stenciled decoration will stand up to the steam and heat of bathrooms very happily, provided that you have started from a good, clean base and that you liberally apply several coats of varnish over the top of your work.

Materials
- Materials
- Iris stencils (see Stencil Templates, page 103)
- Masking tape
- Oil-based stenciling crayons in brown, green, blue, and purple, or colors of your choice
- Size 2, 4 and 6 stenciling brushes
- Glass palette
- Satin or flat aerosol spray varnish

3

3 Begin with some leaves to form the basis for the design. Place them regularly along the top of the wall to be decorated, so you have space to repeat the pattern later. Alternatively, you can place them randomly and fill in with extra leaves at the end.

4 Next add the flowers, using a lighter color on the outside of the flower so darker shading can be added later. Add all the flowers of one type at the same time to keep the balance and insure that there are not too many of one type of flower.

1

1 Make sure your walls are clean, dry, and painted with a flat finish. You will need a suitably sized brush for each color you intend to use.

2 This design is intended to be a more regular pattern, and must therefore be measured carefully. Plan how many flowers you can fit in the space, so you achieve a well-ordered design and avoid any uncomfortable spaces.

2

4

5

5 Now add the second, larger iris stencil to create a more prominent effect to the overall design. Again, use a paler color to the outside of the flowers so they can be shaded.

7 As a finishing touch, fill in any gaps with extra leaves or add a humorous touch, like these bees. Bees or butterflies make very useful extras to fill unwanted spaces in designs with floral or country themes. Paint them using several different colors that tone with the overall design.

An alternative way of obtaining a contrast in the flower's center is to allow the color of the wall to show through. In this case, a white wall gives a pale highlight; however, using a colored wall could be really striking.

ABOVE There are many possible color options, whether you use natural color schemes or not. In this case, both these optional colorways are fairly lifelike, but a strong color scheme in black and silver, or red and orange, could look equally effective in another setting.

6 Here, a darker shading is added to the center of the flowers. This can be a darker tone of the same color, or a contrasting shade to highlight the flowers.

8 Finally, spray the design with varnish to protect it against knocks and scratches. This is particularly important when designs are lower down on a wall. When they are positioned higher up, they are unlikely to get damaged, but at this level the design needs extra protection.

OPPOSITE The irises pick up the colors in both the wallpaper and the rail to make a highly complementary design.

Strawberry Fields

Decorating a Child's Bureau

Pieces of furniture are wonderful objects to decorate, because their appearance can be dramatically altered and adapted to a particular decor. Although a child's bureau has been chosen for this project, you could use any other similar object you like. Even the most plain and inexpensive item can look elegant, countrified, or ultra-modern, depending on the paint effect you choose. Many pieces of furniture can be purchased at a very low cost from thrift stores, rummage sales, or from family members. With a few hours of work, a lot of elbow grease, and a little flair, you can turn a dull piece of furniture into the focal point of a room.

Many different styles of furniture are suitable for stenciled decoration, and looking for suitable pieces can become an enjoyable hobby in itself. The first criteria when choosing a piece to decorate is obviously whether there is a flat area free for decoration. Take careful note of the spaces between handles or other raised decoration, because this impedes the free flow of designs, and more planning and measuring will be necessary. Often a simple, basic piece can be the perfect candidate for stenciling, as other three-dimensional decorations, such as elaborate moldings, do not intrude.

Once you have decided on the piece you wish to decorate, whether it is old or new, you must make sure that the surfaces are all smooth and painted the color that you want for your background (see page 11). If your furniture is an old secondhand piece, then you may need to strip off the old paint, sand down the surface, and stain or paint the wood. Otherwise, you may just need to clean and repaint the item before decorating it. When painting prior to stenciling, always leave lots of time for the paint to dry. If you stencil too soon after painting, the design may blister or lift off.

After you have planned the decoration details and carried out the stenciling, you must finish the painted areas with several good coats of varnish. I always use a spray varnish, because its easy handling insures that no smudging or running of the paint occurs. Repeated coats of varnish are particularly essential on a piece that would receive a fair amount of wear and tear, such as a dining-room chair or kitchen cupboard. Pieces like the bureau pictured here would obviously receive a reasonable amount of use around the handle area, but the sides of the bureau might need fewer coats of varnish. The choice of varnish finish is really a matter of personal preference.

Materials

- Natural wood bureau
- Strawberry stencils (see Stencil Templates, page 103)
- Oil-based stenciling crayons in red, green, and blue, or colors of your choice
- Size 2 stenciling brushes
- Glass palette
- Satin or flat aerosol spray varnish

1 Make sure your piece of furniture is properly prepared for stenciling. A natural unfinished wood bureau was used here, but you could also use one that has been painted with a latex paint. You will need enough brushes for each color, and you will need to plan the placement of your decoration.

2 Paint the green leaves onto the longer drawers using the full stencil. You can either paint the stencil centrally between the two handles, or extend the decoration the entire length of the drawer.

3 Paint the leaves onto the smaller drawers at the top of the chest. Either cut a stencil in half or mask off some of the leaves (see page 14), so you do not smudge any green paint where it is not required.

4 Add the red strawberries onto the drawer fronts. Although red automatically comes to mind when using a well-known fruit like strawberries, the design can look equally effective if you use dark purple, as if the berries were blackberries, or a mixture of white and red to look like unripe strawberries.

5

6 When the entire bureau is finished, spray the decorated drawer fronts liberally with varnish to protect the painted area against any wear it may be subjected to.

6

Helpful Tips
● When using tiny stencils, like the strawberry ones here, use size 2 stenciling brushes. If you try to use a larger brush with such a small stencil, you may slip and cover areas you wanted to keep clear.

OPPOSITE These sweet little strawberries add a fresh country feel to a child's bureau. For a more rustic look, use a wheat and flower stencil.

BELOW Other colorways can all look equally stunning, but bear in mind the color of your background. If you are painting on stained wood, use a strong color that will contrast well. Lighter pastels would show up well against a pale-colored painted bureau.

5 Paint some small butterflies onto the design using a contrasting color, like the blue chosen here, so they show up well against the wood. Other accents could be added, such as small bees or birds.

RIGHT The design can be as simple or as complex as you like, and you can increase the amount of stenciling by adding extra berries or more butterflies.

Ribbon Garland

Applying Pretty Detailing to a Vanity Table

Pretty stenciled images can turn a plain or utilitarian piece of furniture into a real delight. This vanity table has a mirror which makes careful planning necessary, but the design is easy-to-execute and takes very little time to do; the resulting effect makes the table look so much more attractive than when it was plain white.

To plan a theme in a bedroom, or any room, use a color or pattern from one of your already-existing interior decorations for inspiration. For example, use a blue ribbon or a floral motif from a bedspread or quilt as your design, and repeat it throughout the room with decorative touches here and there to match. If there are plain lampshades beside the bed, then a ribbon or flower could be stenciled on them to match your walls, or you could stencil the design on a bedspread or pillows. Matching pillows can also be decorated and placed on a nearby chair, and wide mirror or picture frames lend themselves well to decoration. I am not suggesting that all these bedroom elements should be decorated, but a small selection of them will tie the color scheme together well.

To prepare the surface of your piece of furniture for stenciling, see pages 11 and 32. Take great care when stenciling small, narrow or difficult-to-reach spaces on your furniture. You will need a very small detailed stencil, which may be tricky to place in position and may not look as effective as you intend. If you have a small area that you feel needs a touch of color, then you may find it better to settle for a single leaf or tiny bow to match or complement your design, rather than trying to repeat a scaled-down version of your whole design.

To try an alternative method of decorating to the one shown here, use reverse stenciling. To do this, attach cardboard cut-outs of a simple motif, such as ivy leaves, in a pattern on the areas you wish to decorate. Then spray-paint the entire piece of furniture with a color that contrasts with your background color, such as a Wedgewood blue if your base is white or cream. When the paint has dried, carefully remove the cut-outs, and you will have an ivy leaf design, but with white on blue rather than the reverse. This technique can be achieved by using natural products, too, such as pressed leaves and flowers.

To improve the longevity of your painted decoration, you can, of course, spray with varnish. However, another good idea is to protect the top of the vanity table with a sheet of glass.

1 Before you start, make sure your vanity table is prepared for stenciling. You will need enough brushes for each color you will use, and you will need to measure and mark where you want to place the stencils, keeping balance in mind.

Materials
- Vanity table, painted in white latex
- Ribbon and bow, ivy, and floral stencils (see Stencil Templates, page 103)
- Oil-based stenciling crayons in pink, green, and blue, or colors of your choice
- Size 2 stenciling brushes
- Glass palette
- Satin or flat aerosol spray varnish

2 Begin by stenciling the top surface. The ribbons can be stenciled in one color only, such as the pink here, or darker shading can be added to the streamers or central knot.

3 Paint in the ivy leaves in green. These leaves can also be shaded with a slightly darker color. Small tendrils and berries can be added to give extra length to the design, or a few single extra leaves can be used to fill in odd corners or parts of the object that can not take the entire length of the stencil.

4 Add small, flowery details around the ribbons in blue. Using several different colors for these smaller flowers would also look stunning, but you will need a steady hand and tiny brushes to keep the colors from running together and blending.

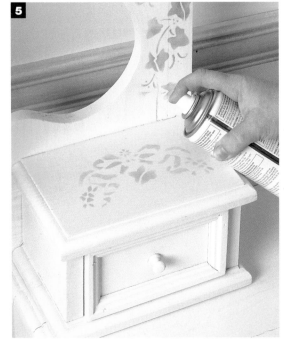

5 When the design is finished, spray all the painted areas really well with the varnish to protect the surface. If you wish, the top surface of the vanity table could be covered with a sheet of glass to shield the paint effect from damage.

LEFT Ivy is an ideal motif to use as a stencil because it is a trailing plant and can have leaves added or taken away without affecting its appearance. This gives you complete flexibility when decorating difficult areas that have limited room for maneuvering.

OPPOSITE A plain, white vanity table becomes an exquisite piece of furniture with a little stenciling. The soft colors accentuate the elegant woodwork.

Individual ivy leaves have been added to the bow and smaller flower designs to give a bolder, heavier decoration to the corners of the vanity tabletop. Make sure that the treatment you give one corner is repeated on other corners, so you achieve an appropriate symmetry.

Rabbits and Balloons

Adding Fun Features to a Child's Toy Box

A large wooden chest or toy box makes a wonderful blank canvas on which to create a fantastic stenciled effect. You can use either one really large design that will cover the top and possibly the sides of the box, or, as in this project, a collection of smaller designs to give a random decorative effect.

Using a collection of different stencils can be a fun way to decorate a plain toy box. If the child is interested in dogs or cats, then a selection of various breeds and colors make a lovely display. Likewise, a selection of train engines and associated images would please a railway enthusiast. An effective design can be created by tracing large block capitals from newspaper headlines to make your stencils, and covering the box with gaily-colored letters randomly placed all over the surfaces – some touching each other and others a little way apart. An even more simple decoration could be achieved with large and small spots. To do this, make stencils in various sizes of circles by tracing around the bases of cups or small bowls, then stencil brightly colored or pastel dots all over the toy box. Another similar idea is to make stencils of simple shapes, such as squares, circles, diamonds, stars, and hearts, and use these to decorate the toy box.

Old chests, trunks, and boxes can be found fairly inexpensively at flea markets and thrift stores. You will need to prepare the surface well (see pages 11 and 32). Remember to clean and paint the inside thoroughly, especially if the box is to be used for storing toys, linen, or other objects. Covering the inside with some lining paper is a good idea for those containers that are to be used as linen chests, as the paper can be replaced as often as you like. For a more decorative effect, line the inside of the box with fabric, gluing the fabric in place along all the edges.

I find the oil-based crayons the best paint for this type of project. The range of subtle colors that can be achieved by using lighter or heavier pressure is highly effective. You may prefer to use other paints, such as small cans of latex paint, but they do not produce the same shaded look. For a bright, fun approach, use gouache paints in vivid or metallic colors. Do remember with any project that is going to be heavily used, particularly by children, to apply several coats of varnish over the design. If your painted box does become damaged, you can retouch the paint, or even plan a new decoration if the old design becomes too battered and worn to save.

Materials

- Wooden toy box, painted in cream latex paint
- Selection of rabbit and alphabet, or name stencils
- Oil-based stenciling crayons in yellow, green, blue, and red, or colors of your choice
- Size 2 and 4 stenciling brushes
- Glass palette
- Satin or flat aerosol spray varnish

1 Make sure your box is prepared for stenciling. You will need suitably sized brushes for each color, and you will need to make a rough plan of where you want to place the stencils.

Helpful Tips

● To find suitable letters for a name stencil, use newspaper headlines. Cut out the letters required and paste them onto a sheet of rigid card stock, and then cut the stencil out (see pages 12–13). If you have a computer, you could also use or adapt a font to create an individualized template – just print out your work at the appropriate size, or enlarge it by photocopying, and cut the stencil! Alternatively, buy a stencil that gives you the entire alphabet.

3 Paint in the name first, using a bold color that will show up well, such as the red chosen here. Alternatively, paint each letter of the name in a different color, but if you do this, use a small brush to help you keep the colors separate.

2 If you are planning to add your child's name to the top of the box, you must measure accurately to insure that the name is exactly central and level (see page 16). Or, place the name off-center to the bottom left or in another position that does not require such precise planning.

When you are stenciling rabbits or other motifs onto the side of a box, you may find it easier to lightly tape the stencil on with masking tape. This will hold it in position and free up your left hand.

Helpful Tips
● Once you have made a template of the letters in your child's name, this could be reduced or enlarged on a photocopier to use on other projects, such as lunch-boxes, school satchels, or shoe bags.

5 After you have covered the toy box with your decoration and it is dry, spray the entire box with at least one coat of varnish, but preferably two. An item like a toy box will receive very rough treatment, and the more protection you can give your handiwork the better!

4 Paint in the rabbits randomly all over the box, using a variety of different stencils and colors. A further selection of animals, such as a collection of zoo or circus animals, would also look attractive and fun.

OPPOSITE Happy little rabbits in different shapes and sizes brighten up this toy box, but you could use any other animal or motif you like.

Creeping Periwinkle

Personalizing a Design for a Child's Chair

Children greatly enjoy personalized designs and gifts. They feel very strongly about their name, as indeed we all do, so decorating an object with a child's name usually gets enthusiastic reactions. The letters used can be bought as precut stencils, or can be made up into a stencil by tracing newspaper or magazine headlines.

Where you place your ornamentation ,and the theme you use, will obviously vary with the type of chair you are decorating. If you are stenciling a chair with little or no decorative woodwork on the back, then you have more scope for design work than on the chair shown in this project, where the back can only take minimal decoration. To stencil a name on the back of the chair, either the front or back side, you will first need to measure and mark the position of the letters, centering the name carefully.

As with other objects that may have awkward areas to stencil, a floral design is often easier to use on a chair (see page 24). If you choose a precise geometric pattern, you will have to plan and measure your design carefully to make sure it fits the chair exactly.

Look for chairs at garage sales or flea markets. Chairs that are discarded by one person can often be joyfully rescued by another, and

you may be lucky enough to find a suitable piece that has been left for garbage collection. Any type of chair, including metal chairs, is worth considering, and you would be surprised at the effects possible with a rejected chair, a little paint, and a stencil or two.

Completely sanding and refinishing a secondhand chair is important. Metal chairs can be sprayed with a flat-finish metal paint, and wooden chairs can be stained or painted. Both finishes look attractive, but you should take your other furniture and interior decoration into consideration. The same basic steps for decorating the child's rocking chair in this project can be used to decorate any other type of chair, such as wooden folding chairs, kitchen chairs and stools, or dining-room chairs.

For an alternative version of the project here, stencil a design onto one of the "director's" chairs that replicate the type of chair a Hollywood director uses. These chairs are available in adult and child sizes, and are constructed from a wooden frame slung with canvas. You will need to use fabric paint to stencil onto the canvas, but the results look extremely effective, and the decorated chair would make a wonderful gift.

Materials
- Child's rocking chair, painted in white latex paint
- Selection of floral stencils, including a name stencil
- Oil-based stenciling crayons in light blue, dark blue, and green, or colors of your choice
- Size 2 stenciling brushes
- Glass palette
- Satin or flat aerosol spray varnish

1 Before you start, make sure your chair is prepared for stenciling. You will need enough brushes for each color you intend to use. Plan where you want to place the stencils, particularly the name stencil, and make light pencil marks in the correct positions.

2 Start with the seat of the chair, and paint a twisting rail of green leaves around the seat. How heavily you decorate the chair is up to you – you might like to paint the edge of the seat and the chair legs, too.

3 Add some periwinkle flowers to the spray of leaves that you have painted onto the seat. The flowers can be all the same color, as demonstrated here, or a gaily colored mixture of shades to make the finished effect brighter.

Helpful Tips
- If you are trying to decorate a rocking chair, it is sometimes very tricky to keep the chair still because it can tip away from you at the crucial moment! Place one or two small wooden wedges under the rockers to keep the chair balanced while you work on it. This will save you a great deal of time – and temper!

LEFT Children love to see their name on their belongings. If you want to add further details, such as a date of birth, then the name could be painted onto the front of the chair and a date of birth added to the back.

4 Next decorate the back of the chair with the child's name, using one color for the whole name, or several different colors if you prefer.

RIGHT The seat of the rocking chair will obviously receive a great amount of rubbing and wear, so you may like to add a second or third coat of varnish after you have finished your stenciling.

5 Spray all the decorated areas of the rocking chair thoroughly with varnish to help protect against the amount of wear and tear the chair is bound to receive.

OPPOSITE Flower stencils look charming on rocking chairs for little girls. You might like to adapt the design for a boy by using nautical themes, which are softly attractive yet definitely masculine.

RIGHT Here is another color scheme you may like to choose for this project. Otherwise, you could use the child's favorite colors, or colors that match the playroom or nursery where the chair will be placed.

Garden Ivy

Revamping Old Wooden Trays

The project here uses a set of wooden trays, which could easily be found among odds and ends at auctions and antique markets. Other types of trays could also be used; for example, an inexpensive metal tray could be painted with a flat-finish spray paint or a flat metal paint, and then stenciled. Many people have old trays they rarely use because they are a little scratched and worn, and these could be repainted and given a new lease of life.

Several good base coats of paint are of paramount importance. If the tray is a dark color and you are painting it a light color, then more coats may be needed to cover the old color or pattern. Once the base coats have been painted and the surface is sufficiently smooth (you may have to sand it down lightly), you are ready to begin stenciling.

Trays must be able to withstand spills, because they are most commonly used to carry beverages, so make sure you choose a suitably protective varnish to coat your finished design. Carefully varnish the entire tray at least two or three times. You may also like to cover the bottom of the trays with baize or felt to prevent the trays from scratching table surfaces.

Flowers, leaves, and garden themes are easy design choices for trays, because they provide an attractive multi-purpose decoration. However, if you have a special color scheme or theme in your kitchen (or the room in which you will use the trays the most), then this can be repeated on the trays. Another possibility is to trace a motif from the china that you would use regularly on the tray onto a stencil. If, for example, you have a pretty rose design on your teapot or china mugs, then use the rose pattern as the basis for your stencil design, adding a few leaves and stems to extend and embellish the design.

You could also decorate the trays with random repeated patterns, such as a simple triangle in various sizes, a teapot shape in different colors, or the word "TEA" in various lettering styles. A flower-bed design could be positioned so one long side of the tray acted as the flower-bed, with various plants rising toward the top of the other long side, and a butterfly or bee floating in the "sky." You may also like to make a matching cloth for the tray, repeating the same stencil decoration or a small motif from the whole design. To do this, use a plain cotton cloth and fabric paints, and follow the instructions for Kitchen Flowers on pages 88-90.

LEFT Here, the ivy design is painted in red and brown to give a completely different effect. You might like to first experiment with different colors and shading on heavy paper or on a surface similar to the tray; this will allow you to create your own unique color scheme.

1 Make sure you have enough brushes in suitable sizes for each color. Decide whether you are going to use the same motif or different ones for all your trays, and then prepare your trays for stenciling.

Materials
- Wooden trays, painted in a pale latex paint
- Ivy stencils (see Stencil Templates, page 103)
- Oil-based stenciling crayons in a range of greens and blues, or colors of your choice
- Size 2 and 4 stenciling brushes
- Glass palette
- Satin or flat aerosol spray varnish

2 Begin by painting on the trails of ivy using a pale green paint. A darker green color will be added as shading later on.

3 When you feel you have enough ivy leaves around the tray, use the shading stencil to add a darker green tinge to the leaves in the middle and on some of the edges. You could also add some dark brown or reddish shading, if you prefer.

4 Add some more detail to the design with sprays of berries and stems. These are painted here in green, but they could just as easily be black or brown to give added contrast.

Helpful Tips
● For trays and other objects that will need to be wiped, you could spray them with a single, thorough coat of varnish, and then, when the first coat is dry, paint a second coat of a more substantial varnish onto the surface with a brush.

5 Finally, paint in some blue butterflies. These add a feeling of lightness and pretty detailing to the design.

6 When the trays are decorated, spray them very thoroughly with several coats of varnish. Because they will be well used, they need a really good coating of varnish to protect your artwork.

OPPOSITE These delightful ivy-covered trays turn an afternoon tea in the garden into a really special occasion.

Terra-cotta Hearts

Painting Flowerpots and Planters

Decorated flowerpots make very attractive gifts, with or without plants, and the plain terra-cotta plant pot is not expensive. You can choose from tiny pots for miniature plants to large planters. Some of the pots are sold with saucers to hold excess water, and these can be decorated to tie in with the design on the flowerpot.

Oil-based stencil paints show up very well on unglazed terra-cotta. The only drawback is the depth of color in terra-cotta, and a paler plaster flowerpot would give you a lot more scope for choosing colors. If you wish to use a terra-cotta pot, but do not want to include the deep terra-cotta color in your overall color scheme, simply paint the flowerpots with several base coats of a colored latex paint. The effect can be very striking; for example, a selection of large cream-colored planters with green frondy plant designs on them would look wonderful in a sunroom, or on a porch or patio.

Large terra-cotta planters and containers that are to be used outside can be decorated, but they will need some all-weather protection. Because painting varnish directly onto a design with a brush can cause the colors to smudge, I recommend using two coats of a spray

varnish over the stenciled design first, before covering the entire object with yacht varnish or another finish suitable for outdoor use. Setting the design first with a spray varnish will prevent any smudges or smears occurring.

You can also decorate other terra-cotta objects, such as kitchen storage jars and crockery, in the same way as the flowerpots. If the objects are to be used in the kitchen, they should be varnished to protect the design against the damaging effects of grease and dust.

Decorated flowerpots can also be used to present other gifts. The pots can be filled with flowering plants, or fresh or dried flower arrangements. A collection of decorated flowerpots, gardening accessories, and seeds would make a fabulous gift for a keen gardener. A large wide-necked terra-cotta bowl could be decorated with a fruit or vegetable stencil, and then used to present a lovely collection of fresh fruit or vegetables. Smaller pots can be gilded around the edges, stenciled with gold paint, and then filled with homemade chocolates or cookies. The flowerpots can also be matched to your interior decoration; for example, if your kitchen is blue and white, you may like to decorate a white painted pot with blue motifs, and use the pot for growing herbs.

Materials

- Plain terra-cotta pots in sizes of your choice
- Heart, star, and bow stencils (see Stencil Templates, page 103)
- Oil-based stenciling crayons in red, blue, and gold, or colors of your choice
- Size 2 and 4 stenciling brushes
- Glass palette
- Satin or flat aerosol spray varnish

1 Using your first color, and holding the stencil firmly with your left hand (or right hand if you are left-handed), paint a few hearts randomly onto the plain terra-cotta flowerpot. You will need to use quite a strong color, like the red shown here, to counteract the orangey terra-cotta background.

2 Using the second color, blue, and using the same heart stencil, add some more hearts to your pot, overlapping them onto the first hearts slightly. You may like to keep the heart motifs separate, or to create a band of hearts around the top and bottom of the flowerpot.

Hearts are one of the most popular design images, and have a long tradition in folk art decoration. The heart is used here in an attractive overlapped effect, and you could repeat this design idea with hearts in varying sizes. You could also use the hearts in a more ordered composition, painting them in one solid color and adding an outline in gold or another color.

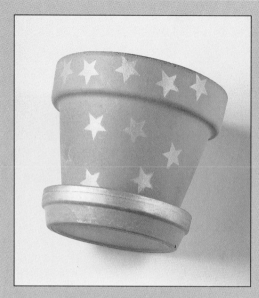

LEFT Here, a terra-cotta saucer has been decorated with a ring of gold. There is not enough space to decorate the saucer with stars to match the flowerpot, but the use of the gold color links the two pieces together well.

LEFT A pretty purple ribbon adorns this flowerpot, and the pot would look attractive holding a plant in a bathroom or bedroom. The bow stencil is rather long, and consequently a little trickier to hold in position while you are stenciling, so take a little more care than usual when applying the paint.

3 Using a third distinct color, antique gold in this case, add some more hearts. Gold and silver both stand out against the terracotta background.

4 Give the flowerpot a good coat of spray varnish. If you want to make the design weatherproof for outdoor use, spray varnish the pot first, and then paint several thicker coats of an outdoor varnish on top.

OPPOSITE Decorated terra-cotta pots can be used indoors and out, and make individual, attractive, and inexpensive gifts.

Fruit and Vegetables

Creating a Recipe Box File for the Kitchen

Looking for unusual ideas for presents can be time-consuming, and this project would make a perfect gift for someone who loves to cook. The project uses a basic cardboard box without dividers or index cards; the cards were later purchased from a stationery store. Paper-based products are very satisfying to decorate, because you can create a completely unique project for very little expense. You may want to extend this project to other forms of paper products, such as writing paper, notepads, or envelopes (see pages 68 and 72).

The box could be given with recipes included on the cards or the cards could be blank, depending on your enthusiasm at the time! If you are decorating a recipe box and collecting recipes for yourself, then duplicating the project for another person is easy. Each divider could be decorated to illustrate different sections; for example, stencil a chicken on the poultry recipe section, a carrot on the vegetable section, or a cow or sheep on the meat section. Alternatively, you could just decorate each divider (or card, if you are feeling ambitious) with a simple leaf, flower, or herb.

The box file does not have to be used as a recipe file. You could use it as a card index for business contacts and decorate it with a more

abstract pattern in stronger colors. The box could be used for indexing collectibles too; many of these items, such as antique cutlery or books, lend themselves to interesting decorative motifs.

The recipe box used here is covered with brown paper, so you can use a variety of different paints on the surface. Water-based ink pads are a good choice, the oil-based stencil crayon, as used here, are very successful, and other watercolor or acrylic paints are suitable, too. Felt-tip pens can also be applied through a stencil if you like the effect they create, and these are ideal for children to use.

Remember that with a dark-colored background as the base color, you will need to use colors that are slightly brighter than if the background had been white or cream. Obviously, if you would prefer a lighter background, paint the box with several coats of latex paint in a color of your choice. When you are base-coating items for stenciling, make sure you use a flat-finish paint. Paint will not adhere properly to glossy finishes, unless you use special car spray paints which can be tricky to use. The box will be handled a fair bit, so finish with a coat of spray varnish to set the design and protect the paint against wear.

Materials

- A cardboard box and set of plain index cards
- Fruit and vegetable stencils (see Stencil Templates, page 103)
- Oil-based stenciling crayons in green, yellow, brown, and red, or colors of your choice
- Size 2 stenciling brushes
- Glass palette
- Satin or flat aerosol spray varnish

1 Before you start, make sure you have enough brushes for each color you intend to use. If the only boxes you can find are too brightly colored, or have an unsuitable surface, then you can cover them in brown paper or even a light-colored handmade paper. Use plenty of glue to make sure that the paper is completely and evenly stuck down all over the box.

2 Plan your design so it fits exactly onto the sides and top of the recipe box file. To extend the stencil, you could add another bunch of vegetables, or you could remove a bunch to make the design smaller.

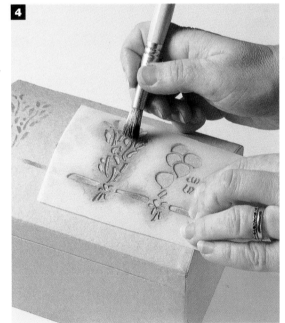

3 Stencil each bunch separately in a different color to give a good contrast. To produce a shadow and add a little three-dimensional quality to the design, use a darker color to shade the onions on one side.

4 Use a small brush to paint on the more intricate details, making sure that the area is completely covered and the colors are kept separate. Either paint the vegetables their authentic color, or use a little artistic license to add alternative colors to the design.

5 Next paint the tops of the bunches a leafy green. The design will look more striking if you choose bold, definite colors, particularly if you are using a box with a brown finish, like the one here.

7 Finally, spray the entire recipe box with varnish to protect it from knocks and spills in the kitchen.

6 To add interest to the design, paint some details on each vegetable bunch, such as dots on the corn or veins on the onions. Repeat the whole process on the sides of the box.

OPPOSITE Fruit, herbs, vegetables, and other kitcheny motifs transform a recipe box file and dividers.

BELOW Although realistic colors may seem the obvious choice for this project, purple carrots might brighten up the recipe box, or use a completely blue color scheme to match a blue kitchen.

BOTTOM The divider cards inside the recipe box can also be decorated with single bunches of ingredients to match the exterior of the box.

Ribbons and Tulips

Making a Beautiful Wooden Jewelry Box

Small boxes are fun to work on and very successful items to decorate. Boxes are available in many shapes and sizes, heart-shaped, round, square, or triangular, and they can all look beautiful with some stenciled motifs added. They make excellent jewelry boxes, but also good gift boxes for other presents.

Boxes and containers to decorate can be obtained from many different sources. Although attractive containers can be bought, you can use simple cardboard boxes from previous gifts or even left-over packaging from food ingredients. Tin cans can be painted with enamel paints, and glass jars can be given a base coat of latex paint. A large coffee jar, painted with several coats of flat latex paint, can be decorated with some very pretty stencil work to make an attractive container for the kitchen or bathroom. Light wooden round boxes, such as those used to package cheese, can be painted and decorated, and many other possibilities may occur to you when you look in your cupboards.

When choosing your box to decorate, remember that a flat surface is easiest to stencil on, and curved or semi-circular lids or surfaces can be very much harder. Try to choose a container that is square, particularly if this is your first attempt at stenciling, or a box with a flat lid.

Any flat surface can be decorated, such as a painted cardboard box or a painted wooden surface, as with this project.

Planning your composition carefully is imperative, and you may want to trace your design lightly onto the box before you actually begin applying paint. Scale is an important factor to consider – the design should be planned so it fits neatly onto the box, leaving some space around the edges. Should you decide to decorate the box with a border design, then you must calculate carefully how the four corners will fit together. A decorative geometric border, such as small diamonds set in squares, is not difficult to produce, and you may find it best to measure your box first and then alter the stencil to fit.

Small random motifs are usually the easiest way to add some decoration to a box, and the random pattern will allow you to avoid problems with corners matching. However, do not try to stencil a very tiny design; unless the stencil is beautifully and very meticulously cut, a well-defined and clear image is difficult to achieve. Remember also that boxes are made to be opened, and the inside of the box can be stenciled to add interest. Even just a small motif on the inside of the lid is striking and unexpected.

1 Make sure the surface of your box is prepared and you have the correct number of brushes for each color you want to use. Plan your design, measuring and marking where you want to place the stencils.

2 Place the stencil in the appropriate position on the top of the box, and start by stenciling the ribbons in blue. If you want to expand the design to fit a larger box, the ribbons can be elongated by adding extra tails or streamers.

Materials
- A plain wooden jewelry box, painted in pink latex paint
- Ribbon and tulip stencils
- Oil-based stenciling crayons in red, green, and blue, or colors of your choice
- Size 2 stenciling brushes
- Glass palette
- Satin or flat aerosol spray varnish

3 Next paint in the leaves and flowers. Choose colors, like the green and red here, that give a good contrast to the ribbon; otherwise, the leaves and ribbons can become indistinguishable from each other.

5 If desired, add a small design inside the lid. Here, a stencil has been created that is very similar to the one on the lid, but it has only one tulip instead of several.

OPPOSITE A little treasure chest for jewels is easily created from a painted wooden box and a few simple stencils.

LEFT Here is the same stencil, but in a different color. You can repaint your box any color you choose to create a background that is sympathetic to your stencil design.

4 Decorate the sides of the box. Use a different but complementary stencil, like the one here, or continue with the same stencil you have used for the top of the box, perhaps masking off some of the design to use only a small part of the whole stencil (see page 14).

6 Finally, when you have completed all the decoration, varnish the entire box well with the spray varnish. Cover both the inside and outside of the box. Leave the inside and top edges to dry before closing the lid, or the box will stick fast.

Paper Flowers

Customizing Office Supplies and Folders

Decorated files and stationery products make the office a prettier place to work, or home-filing more fun. The standard files used in this project are available from large stationer's or office stationery suppliers. Try to select the plainest ones you can. Some files have heavy black printing across the flap, which spoils any stenciled designs, so look carefully before you choose your brand of file, and make your selection according to the color that suits your design best. Because painting the surface of the file is not possible, you will be limited to the colors available from your local stationery supplier.

Decorating paper products means you can use a variety of paints, either water-based ink pads, watercolor paints, or the oil-based stenciling crayons. You could also consider acrylics or other mediums. I prefer the water-based ink pads, used in conjunction with the sponge applicators, or the oil-based crayons. As a precaution, spray the finished design with a light varnish, using either the standard variety or a special artist's fixative available from art and craft suppliers.

Decorating ordinary items, such as box files and folders, immediately makes them a possible gift item. If you are creating your own

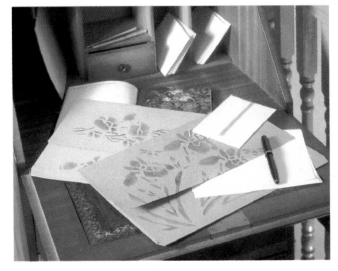

stencils, use your imagination and consider the person who will be receiving the object. For example, a box file decorated with flowers and flowerpots could be filled with seed packets and tips torn from gardening magazines, and this would please any avid gardening enthusiast. Father's Day presents could be solved by decorating a large file for home-office use, with motifs taken from his favorite sport or hobby. Sports cars and racing flags could decorate the file of a car enthusiast, and reels, hooks, and various sizes of fish could decorate the file of a fisherman.

Children may also be amused to receive personalized folders for their homework or exam notes, and you could incorporate their names into the design, as well as images from their interests and hobbies. Another idea is to decorate the folder according to the contents; for example, a file for electricity bills could be decorated with light bulbs, or a cook's recipe folder could be stenciled with fruit and vegetables. Once you are underway with a folder project, you will find it easy to repeat your designs on stationery, blank postcards, or other notepaper. You could even use a special stencil as your own personal logo to decorate your headed stationery or letter-writing paper.

Materials

- Assorted office folders
- Poppy stencils (see Stencils, page 103)
- Oil-based stenciling crayons in red, green, gray, and brown, or colors of your choice
- Size 2 and 4 stenciling brushes
- Glass palette

1 Make sure you have a suitably sized brush for each color you want to use. The composition is simple enough not to need any advance planning.

3 Next stencil the poppies using a strong red color. Shade a little toward the edges of the petals by applying more pressure to get a darker coloring.

Helpful Tips

● As an alternative to oil-based stencil crayons, you could use the water-based ink pads for this project. Apply the ink with sponges or sponge applicators.

2 Position the stencil on the folder and paint in the stalks and leaves. Depending on your taste, you can either just decorate the flap for a more minimal design, or cover the entire folder for more profuse poppies.

4 Add the poppy heads in gray or brown, and also shade the center of the poppies with the same color. Adding shading gives more depth to the design and looks far more effective.

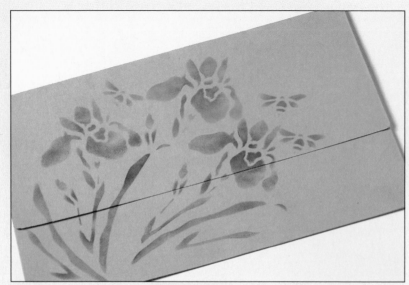

RIGHT A very strong design is created here using an iris stencil in strong pinks and mauves. A few bees have been added in a mauve color, and they help intensify the pretty colors in this decoration.

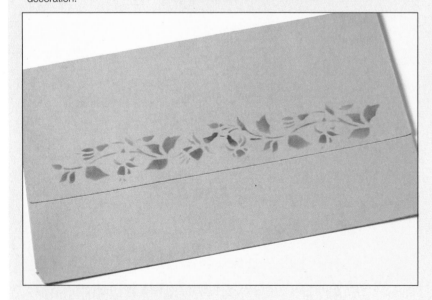

LEFT Here the folders have been decorated in a much more minimal fashion, with a neat line of fuchsias across the edge of the flap. If you are decorating a selection of folders, you may like to make some much bolder in both color and composition than others.

ABOVE The same poppy stencil has been used here, but with different colors. The yellow color scheme would be less successful on a darker background, such as pink folders.

OPPOSITE Pretty poppy and iris folders add a feminine touch to office or personal organization, but you could adapt the idea by using any stencil you prefer. A border around the edges of the folders would also transform these ordinary items.

Purple Columbine

Making Wrapping Papers and Gift Tags

Wrapping paper is always a great expense, especially at Christmas time when there are so many presents to wrap. The paper is usually ripped off the gifts and simply thrown away. Why then do we pay such vast sums for sheets and rolls of beautiful paper when a much prettier and more economical solution is right under our noses?

Brown paper or cream drawer lining paper is very well suited to stenciling, and can work with ink pads, watercolors, acrylics, and stenciling crayons. The paper is available by the roll and works out relatively inexpensively. If you invest in a large roll, then suitably sized sheets can be torn off and used individually. Working this way allows for flexibility and gives you an opportunity to create different designs on each sheet as you need it.

If you are creating your own stencils for gift-wraps, there are many images you could use. Designs for children's wrapping papers could include traditional motifs, such as teddy bears, lambs, drums, cars, or dolls, or more abstract patterns, such as squiggles or shapes in bright colors. For animal-lovers, choose cats, dogs, fish, or wild animals, depending on personal tastes. Flowers are always a safe choice, because they are popular and appropriate for almost every occasion.

If you are stenciling some sheets just for "stock" supplies, so you have some paper handy when the need arises, then flowers are one of the best themes. Ivy, roses, and honeysuckle work well, but other suitable ideas include hearts, polka dots, and ribbons and bows.

A vast range of striking images are suitable for Christmas paper, such as holly and ivy, poinsettias, wreaths, and angels. Stars and other simple shapes look highly effective when painted in gold and silver, and a Christmas tree is an easy image to trace when creating a stencil. Christmas trees could be stenciled all over the paper in shades of green and gold to produce a festive gift-wrap. Although many festive stencils are commercially available, making your own is a fun project during the holiday season. Search through old Christmas cards for motifs to make up into stencils.

To make matching gift tags, cut a rectangle from the brown or cream paper and fold it in half. Stencil a small image onto one side, and thread some ribbon or string through the corner to attach the tag to the gift. Take care to choose a small stencil when decorating the matching tag, or else reduce the size of your wrapping paper design to create a new, smaller stencil (see page 12).

Materials
- Brown packaging paper
- Green string or raffia
- Floral stencils (see Stencil Templates, page 103)
- Oil-based stenciling crayons in green and purple, or colors of your choice
- Size 2 and 4 stenciling brushes
- Glass palette

1 Make sure you have a brush for each color. The easiest and often most effective way to create wrapping paper is to place the stencil randomly, so advance planning is not really necessary.

3 Paint in the flower using bold colors to counteract the dulling effect of the brown background. You can either use the same color for all the flowers, or use several different colors to achieve a multicolored effect.

2 Start with the leaves, positioning the stencil to allow enough room for the flower when that is added at the next stage. Paint in green leaves all over the surface.

Helpful Tips
- As an alternative to brown wrapping paper, you could use cream or white drawer lining paper, or any other inexpensive paper available. Of course, if you want really extravagant wrapping paper for a special occasion, choose among the many beautiful handmade and textured papers that are available from stationers and artist supply stores.

4

OPPOSITE The natural motifs stenciled on these gifts look attractive against the rustic brown paper. For a more graphic effect, use more abstract designs on high-quality colored paper.

ABOVE Delicately colored flowers make a perfect gift-wrap design for a Mother's Day present or a spring wedding gift.

4   Make a matching gift tag by carefully cutting out a rectangle of paper. Fold it in half to make a square, and thread some string, raffia, or thin decorative cord through the corner. You may like to trim the edges with wavy-edged scissors for more decorative effect. The tag can then be stenciled to match the wrapping paper.

RIGHT This technique can be used for all kinds of wrapping papers, from the stenciled Christmas tree and stars gift-wrap shown here, to wrapping papers for birthdays, anniversaries, weddings, christenings, or any other celebration. Floral designs are particularly useful because they are suitable for myriad occasions.

Helpful Hints
● An excellent time-saver is to wrap the gift first and then stencil the flowers straight onto the package in position. This allows you to place the motifs exactly where you want them. With this method, you also avoid discarding those little decorated scraps that are often left over after gifts have been wrapped.

Creative Greetings

Designing Your Own Greeting Cards

Handmade stenciled greeting cards give a tremendous amount of pleasure to the recipient, and they take a minimal amount of time to produce, especially when compared with painting or embroidery. The area where stenciling really comes into its own is on large numbers of identical designs. If you are designing and cutting a stencil for one card only, it can be a little time-consuming, but if you decide to create your own Christmas cards, for example, then a little time invested in planning the design and creating the stencil is soon repaid with the quick and simple production of a large number of cards.

Good-quality card stock or heavyweight paper is important for handmade cards, because a card that bends and collapses when you try to stand it up immediately looks unprofessional. One stumbling block can often be finding an envelope the correct size. The easiest way around this problem is to buy envelopes first, then purchase your card stock or paper in the toning or contrasting colors that you require, and cut the individual cards to fit the envelopes.

Once you have created a stencil, do keep it clean and safe in a clearly labeled folder. At some later date, even if you decide not to use

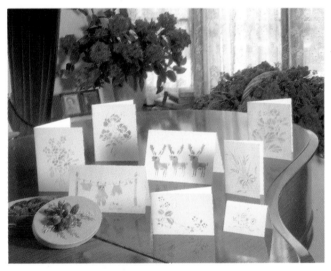

the same stencil again, a part of that design, such as a small bow, leaf, or flower, may be just what you need to fill a space on another project!

Numbers and letters are often useful for greeting cards. A special birthday or anniversary can be commemorated with a card bearing a large 16 or 21. Large letters and numbers can be sourced from newspapers and magazines, making it very simple to personalize a card with a name, number, or date.

Care should be taken with the choice of paints. If you use watercolor or other water-soluble paints, they should be kept very dry, or smudges and smears may spoil the design. Ink pads have been used on all the cards shown here. They are easily available from stationer's, and are excellent for this purpose, because they are very dry and come in a wide range of colors. They can be applied with sponges, small brushes, or even with cotton swabs.

Finally, when planning your designs, remember that stenciling can be used together with other ideas. For example, a bouquet of flowers could be stenciled onto a card and a satin ribbon bow added to give three-dimensional interest. Paper cut-outs, silk flowers, children's erasers, and candies can all become part of a much-appreciated card.

Materials
- Envelopes and pieces of card stock or heavyweight paper, in colors of your choice
- Ink pads, in a selection of colors
- Sponge applicators or small pieces of sponge
- Cotton swabs
- Various stencils

1 Choose the correct size of envelope, cut a piece of card stock or paper, and fold to fit. Plan the design before cutting the stencil. Have several applicators or sponges to hand, using a different applicator for each color.

2 Before making any marks on the card, roughly measure the size of the design, including any repeating patterns. Keep the design away from the edges of the card. Dab or rub across the stencil lightly with ink, applying the color as drily as possible. Repeat the application, if necessary, to achieve the depth of color you require.

3 Even spacing between each animal is important for a professional look. Likewise, the pressure and depth of color on each reindeer should also be similar, unless you wish to make them totally different colors.

4 Once the reindeer are painted, and you are happy with the color, paint in the eyes. Rub a cotton swab onto the ink pad, erring on the side of caution with the amount of color. Dab in the reindeer eyes with the cotton swab.

Helpful Tips
- If your design requires spots or other small areas of color, it is often easiest to use a rigid applicator, such as a cotton swab, rather than a flexible brush. Use a cotton swab to apply spots to animals, balloons, or other features.

5 Complete all the reindeers' eyes. Finally, apply red to Rudolph's nose (the reindeer at the right of the design). All the animals could be given red noses, if you like, or paint black noses on the remaining reindeer.

Helpful Tips

● A successful method of stenciling on cards is to apply the color with a sponge. Sponge applicators are easy to control, making them particularly suitable for painting detailed areas. A small sponge can work equally well; it should be rubbed over the ink pad and then dabbed evenly over the area to be colored.

ABOVE This card would be ideal for a wedding or anniversary. The bell has been sponged with several colors to give an unusual golden yellow and brown effect, and the bow and flowers can be colored to suit the occasion – for example, you may like to color the ribbons gold for a golden wedding anniversary card.

BELOW The delicate shades of sweet peas offer plenty of inspiration for choosing colors. Because these sweet peas have been stenciled onto a green card, stronger colors have been chosen to make sure they stand out. If you use a white or cream card, then paler colors would be equally successful.

OPPOSITE This selection of cards shows only a very small number of the many possible designs you could create. Handmade cards are unique and lend an extra-special touch to all occasions and celebrations.

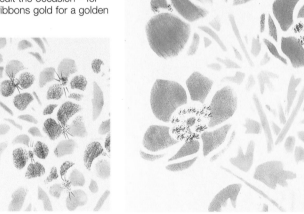

RIGHT Pansies must rate as one of the world's favorite flowers, after the rose. These little heartsease pansies are stenciled in shades of purple and yellow, and would be a safe choice for any friend or relative.

LEFT Bright anemones make a perfect design for a cheering get-well card. There are many vivid colors in the anemone palette that could be used. Here, blue and pink make a striking effect and the black centers stand out strongly.

Memories of the Sea

Decorating Photograph Frames and Mounts

Often photographs lie in an album ignored for years, but if you display your favorite pictures from this year's vacation in a beautiful frame, like the one shown here, they can be admired long after the special event. You can easily change the photographs after your next vacation to update the collection. Of course, the techniques used here can be adapted to produce a frame and mount for any other photographic subject, such as using tiny heart and flower stencils to frame snapshots of children.

Multi-aperture mounts are usually available from craft stores and photography sections in department stores as part of a standard collection. However, the spacing between the openings is usually much tighter than the mount chosen for this project. If you are using a mount with narrow spaces, you will need to use a tiny, delicate design, and stenciling around these areas is actually much more difficult than it might seem. A mount with wider spaces can be cut to your requirements by a specialist picture-framing establishment.

Plain, wide frames are fairly easy to find. A specialist picture framer may be able to help you, but look in large chain stores because a standard range of frames may provide something suitable for this

project. The frame should be as wide, plain, and flat as possible and made of unfinished wood. Many frames have decorative moldings which make adding a stencil design difficult. A frame without woodwork details is simple to stencil on, and unfinished wood takes color well and can be varnished to protect the design. You can sand down a glossy frame, but if the frame is too highly polished or is plastic, this may not be a viable option.

Several coats of varnish must be applied to the frame after stenciling, to protect the design from damage and so you can handle the frame as much as you like to change the photographs inside. If you want to hang the frame on the wall, you will need two screw eyes to secure to the frame so you can attach wire or string across the back. If you want to stand the frame up on a table, you will need a back for the picture with a free-standing strut.

Stenciled frames and mounts also make delightful gifts. You may like to give one of your own creations as a present for someone's birthday, and include cake, candles, and party hats as stencil motifs, along with photographs from previous birthdays. Even special awards or academic degrees can be commemorated in a decorative frame.

Materials

- Plain, wide, unvarnished wooden photo frame
- Mount board with several apertures to fit the frame
- Photographs
- Seashore stencils (see Stencil Templates, pages 103)
- Oil-based stenciling crayons or water-based ink pads in blue, purple, red, and green, or colors of your choice
- Size 2 and 4 stenciling brushes, or sponges
- Glass palette
- Satin or flat aerosol spray varnish

2 Decorate the frame first with your largest stencils, such as the boats and lighthouse used here.

1 Make sure you have suitably sized brushes, or enough sponges, for each color of paint you intend to use. Carefully plan where you want your decoration to go before you commit paint to wood or mount board. The designs should be planned so they are evenly spaced out.

3 Intersperse delicate details among the heavier motifs. Here, a few birds lighten the frame and fill in spaces. When you have finished, put the frame on one side to dry and start work on the mount board.

Helpful Tips

- When you buy or cut the mount board for the frame, make sure that the holes are cut far enough apart to leave plenty of room for your stenciled designs. To cut your own holes, trace appropriate squares or rectangles on the board (circles are difficult to execute and are best avoided). Using a scalpel, metal ruler, and a cutting mat, carefully cut out each shape. Cut in a smooth long line with the blade against the ruler. For a beveled edge, angle the blade at about 60°.

4

5

5 When the frame is dry, spray it well with varnish because it will be handled quite extensively and the varnish will protect the paint effects. The mount, however, does not need to be sprayed because it will be protected behind the glass.

Helpful Tips
● Small pieces of natural or synthetic sponge can also be used as applicators. Because you are working on narrow areas with fairly small stencils, the sponges can be cut to a size that is manageable for you. The color is dabbed on with the sponge – a useful method creating soft coloring.

4 The mount can be stenciled with designs matching the frame, or with complementary motifs as shown here. The marine theme is carried through from the frame to the mount with soft colors.

BELOW The base of the frame is given weight by some buildings which are painted in cheerful colors. Many other features could be included in the design, such as trees, flowers, or beach umbrellas.

BELOW The stenciled motifs can be painted in any color scheme. Here, the blue marine theme has been changed to a bright sunny color scheme, highlighted in yellow and brown.

OPPOSITE Seashore motifs in soft colors add fun to this wooden frame. To add interest, you could also paint the frame a pale color before decorating.

ABOVE Do not use very bright colors on the mount or the photographs will be overwhelmed and will not look their best.

Garden Flowers

Creating Stylish Pillow Covers

Pillow covers can be decorated so easily with a simple stencil and a selection of fabric paints. Fabric paints are absolutely essential, because the standard acrylic, watercolor, or other paints may run and smudge on the fabric. More importantly, fabric paints will enable your finished item to be laundered, which in the case of pillow covers is essential. For more on fabric paints, see pages 10 and 84.

Plain cotton or muslin pillow covers are inexpensive to buy, yet become beautiful hand-painted creations with a little artistic input. Any plain covers can be decorated; the ones used here are unbleached heavyweight muslin that has

been piped with some colored cotton fabric, but you may prefer to use another type of fabric. A relatively smooth fabric, rather than one with too coarse or textured a weave, is easiest to stencil on. You will also find a patterned fabric virtually impossible to stencil successfully, and chintzes or other glazed fabrics are not suitable for this method of decorating. If you feel so inclined, make your own pillows following one of the many patterns available from department stores and specialist sewing stores. You will need to make sure your fabrics are colorfast and preshrunk before you begin sewing and stenciling.

The technique used in this project is also good for bed linen, bedspreads, and throws for beds or sofas. Once you have become proficient with fabric stenciling, the possible projects are endless. However, any heavily-used linen that is going to be washed every week would not be suitable for stenciled decoration. A better option is to use undecorated sheets and pillowcases, and display a hand-stenciled bedspread on top of the bed. Or, place a selection of pretty pastel pillows on the bed that are for ornamental use only. If the pillows are small enough, and the colors work together well, you can use a great variety of different paint effects and designs. The paint effect will withstand machine-washing, but only occasionally, and it is not intended to be subjected to really heavy wear.

There are so many different fabric items that lend themselves to stenciled decoration. With original stencil designs and careful planning, you can create a range of household items that are completely unique and add a new dimension to any room. Often the size of the budget allocated to redecorate a room is not the key to success, and some creative thought and unusual decorative ideas can give a much more satisfactory result.

Materials

- Plain, cotton or muslin pillow covers
- Honeysuckle or other floral stencils
- Fabric paints in yellow ochre, maroon, and green, or colors of your choice
- Size 2 and 4 stenciling brushes
- Glass palette

2 Stencil on the first color. Here a yellow ochre was used for the honeysuckle stencil. Either shade a lighter color into the center, or use the second color you have chosen, such as the maroon shown here.

3 Add the second color onto the flowers. Some could be completely maroon, and some shaded yellow and maroon. More than two colors could be used for the flowers, if you like; for example, a pale pink or peach color could be introduced here.

1 Wash the pillow cover first to insure it is clean and preshrunk, and make sure you have suitably sized brushes for each color you will use. This design is a random pattern, so needs little measuring, but if you choose a geometric pattern, then careful thought and planning should go into the positioning of the stencils.

4 Next add the leaves and stems, twisting them across the pillow. With a naturally trailing design like this honeysuckle here, it is simple to do a randomly spaced pattern.

5 When you have completed the pillow, the fabric paints must be set with an iron. Read the instructions that accompany the fabric paints, because the technique may vary from one manufacturer to another.

Helpful Tips
● If this is your first attempt at using fabric paints, practice on a spare piece of fabric first to make sure you get a feeling for using the paints. Always use less paint than you think necessary, and add a little more later to darken the color.

OPPOSITE Wisteria, iris, and lily designs are painted on these delightful pillows in fabric paints. Before starting, plan your design by choosing a color scheme or design to suit your interior decoration.

LEFT This pretty wisteria design would look lovely in a bedroom or living room. The same design could be used on the walls to create a complete theme for a room, especially if you have wisteria climbing outside one of the windows.

LEFT Choose the color scheme that will blend well with the room in which you intend to use your newly stenciled pillow. You could pick out one main color from a sofa or curtain fabric, or just scatter a range of pretty designs across a bed or chair.

Golden Lilies

Stenciling a Small Tablecloth

This tablecloth shows how an inexpensive fabric, in this case plain muslin, can be transformed into an object of beauty. The small size of this cloth is ideal for a bedside table or circular occasional table that has just enough space for a reading lamp or ornament, but you can decorate any size of tablecloth by following the techniques shown here. A special table is not necessary because it will not be visible beneath the cloth, and chipboard or particle board tables sold as flat packs, and which slot together easily, are ideal. Although the board tables are pretty unattractive when uncovered, you are unaware of the furniture when the cloth is in place.

hemmed square of fabric. The extra benefit in making your own tablecloth is that you can add a trim or edging to the cloth that reflects the stencil decoration or emphasizes one of the colors you have used. If you are skilled at sewing, you could even create a scalloped or other decorative hem to the cloth that follows the pattern of the stenciled border.

Fabric paints are necessary for this project, and they are available in a fairly wide range of colors. The colors show up on the fabric much the same color as they appear in the container, which makes choosing the paints to match your color scheme easy. The colors can be strengthened by painting over a stencil several times, and you can mix the paints to gain new colors; the colors also mix together well when you use one on top of another.

If you can not find a plain muslin tablecloth, there are many plain cotton cloths available in all shapes and sizes, and a colored background might work better with your color scheme. For example, the lily design shown here could be used on a pale gold, primrose yellow, or even a very pale green fabric, and a wisteria design on a pale lilac or mauve background can look absolutely wonderful. Dark backgrounds are very difficult to use successfully, apart from such notable exceptions as gold stars on a navy or black background. A more cost-effective alternative is to make your own tablecloth from a simple

If you do not want to use a floral design, then there are plenty of other possibilities. Do bear in mind the extra bonus when using floral designs: if you have a small space that is not large enough to take a full flower or repeat, you can add odd leaves, stalks, or buds without spoiling the overall effect. This really does make life easier, as exact repeats of a geometric design have a habit of not quite fitting, even though you have carefully measured the item to be stenciled.

Materials
- Plain cotton or muslin circular tablecloth
- Lily or other floral stencils
- Fabric paints in green, yellow, and ochre, or colors of your choice
- Size 4 and 6 stenciling brushes
- Glass palette

1 Wash the tablecloth first, and make sure you have suitably sized brushes for each color. This design is an ordered composition and will need planning to insure that the stencils are evenly spaced.

You can measure the cloth by dividing it into equal sections and marking where the lilies should be placed. To decorate the middle, simply fold the cloth in half, then in half again, to locate the exact center.

2 Apply green fabric paint to the leaf section of the lily stencil, following your marked positions so the flowers are carefully and exactly spaced all around the edge of the tablecloth.

3 Next add a pale color, such as the yellow shown here, for the outside of the petals. This can be shaded toward the center of the flower if you wish. The lilies can be all the same color, or a selection of different colors can be introduced.

4

OPPOSITE This charming tablecloth is decorated in the center, as well as along the edge. If you intend to display items on the table, it is a good idea to protect the cloth with a sheet of glass cut to the size of the table.

4 Then add the darker, ochre color in the center of the flower as shading. This adds depth and interest to the design and helps create a more professional look.

5

LEFT Decorate only the edges of the cloth if you intend to display something on the table that may damage the paintwork. Otherwise, you can stencil a design around a smaller circular area in the center of the cloth.

5 When you have painted the decoration all the way around the base of the cloth and the paints are dry, the design must be set. Carefully read the instructions that accompany the paints, and iron both sides of the cloth to make the design washable.

LEFT For a simple design, stencil only one type of lily around the edge. For a more complex decoration, use smaller lilies and buds, plus a bee or butterfly to expand the design.

Kitchen Flowers

Matching Motifs on Kitchen Accessories

There are many utilitarian kitchen items that can be given a special look with a simple stencil or two. Oven mitts are not very glamorous pieces, but they are a useful and necessary cooking aid. In this project, several varieties of oven mitts and hot pads have been made from a heavyweight muslin and decorated with various floral motifs. Although these items are very simple to make from fabric if you like to sew, plain cotton versions can be purchased and decorated in the same way.

A coordinated set of items for the kitchen looks lovely and makes a wonderful gift. You could give a selection of oven mitts, hot pads, place mats, napkinss, and even an apron as a present. If you enjoy sewing, you may like to make a pad on which to rest hot plates and fill it with herbs and spices so the aroma is released as the pad is warmed. Whatever item you choose to stencil, keep in mind that the decorated items can not be washed frequently.

Because these are kitchen items, you might like to use a food theme for your design, such as vegetables or fruit. Many people have a cow, pig, or other animal theme in the kitchen, and these shapes work really well as stencils and could be repeated on the walls. Other

kitchen accessories can be stenciled too, and toaster or appliance covers look great with a little added color stenciled on. Decorated tea towels or cloths for trays could add a special individual touch to your kitchen, provided they are reserved for limited use.

One of the most striking items to stencil in a kitchen is a roller blind. Roller blinds are completely flat and therefore present no problems in adding a stenciled design. The only knack is getting them to stay open so you can work on them, assuming that you are decorating a ready-made blind rather than using a special kit. Having struggled with two members of my family holding the blind back, I suggest you stretch the blind out on a large table or the floor and weigh the corners down with tin cans or weights from a kitchen scale. This way you will have a firm, flat surface area to work on. Choose themes for your decoration that tie in with your kitchen. Often brighter, bolder patterns look more attractive than dainty designs on blinds. Remember that only part of the decoration will be seen at times, so check that the design looks attractive if only the bottom few inches are showing. Make sure you do not stencil the design upside down and that you work from top to bottom.

1 Make sure the oven mitts and hot pads are clean, and that you have the right brushes for each color you will use. The ivy design is a random pattern, so no planning is needed; however, if you choose a more elaborate stencil, you may like to mark where the stencils will be positioned.

Materials
- Plain cotton or heavyweight muslin oven mitts or hot pads
- Ivy stencil (see Stencil Templates page 103), or any flower stencils of your choice
- Fabric paints in yellow ochre and green, or colors of your choice
- Size 2 and 4 stenciling brushes
- Glass palette

2 Apply the first color onto your chosen accessory; here, green fabric paint is used. You may find it helps to practice on a spare piece of cloth to find the correct amount of paint and pressure to use.

3 Add the shading to the leaves. In this case, a yellow ochre was added to tone down the green and add some variation to the design. Obviously, many other colorways would be equally successful.

4 When you are happy with the design and the paint is dry, read any instructions that accompany your fabric paints. Then iron both sides of the mitt or hot pad to set the paint.

BELOW If you are using a simple design with a minimal number of colors, make sure that enough visual interest is apparent in the design. Details, such as the bee added to this hot pad, can turn a sparse design into something more stunning.

OPPOSITE A range of plain kitchen mitts and hot pads can be given your own individual style with the simple addition of a few stencil motifs.

ABOVE These plain oven mitts have simple daisies stenciled onto them. Other kitchen accessories can be decorated, such as tea towels and egg cozies.

ABOVE These oven mitts are decorated with a design that lends itself to the long shape. Alternatively, you could decorate them with a border all around the edge of the mitts, and add a few flowers in the middle.

Helpful Tips
● Although fabric paints are available in a wide range of colors, it is also possible to create colors by placing a small sample of each color onto your glass palette and mixing them.

Butterflies and Bees

Using Delicate Designs on Voile Curtains

Net or voile curtains are sometimes necessary, particularly if you have a room that overlooks a street. Plain nets can be a little dull, and frilly nets do not always match your style of decor. This project adds an unusual decorative touch to a window, while keeping the privacy that voile curtains can offer.

Voile is available in cream or white, and the choice of color is yours. Always consider the other colors or items in the room. White tends to look more modern, while cream has an older, more antique, look. A simple hem on each end is all that is required, because the curtains can hang on a curtain wire or rod.

Fabric paints are the ideal medium to use on this project, but if you are particularly keen to match the colors used elsewhere in the room, then the oil-based stenciling crayons can be used. Although the curtains will not be washable if you use the crayons, the paints do give a good strong color. Fabric paints, though, are absolutely necessary if your curtains need frequent washing. The best method for applying color to a large piece of fabric is to work on a protected tabletop with chairs at one end to drape the fabric over as you work. You can then simply push the fabric along, and the paint can dry without danger of smudging.

The amount of stenciling you want to add to the curtains is up to you. If you just want to add a pretty touch here and there, then a light scattering of butterflies and bees, as in the project shown here, would be sufficient. If you want to make the curtains considerably darker, a heavily stenciled pattern that covers a fair percentage of the curtain is the best choice for you.

There are so many other designs that would work equally well with this fabric. Keeping the airy feel to the design, you could stencil bluebirds, stars, moons, or suns onto the curtains. Or, you could add a garden theme to the room with a border of flowers along the bottom of the curtain with taller flowers, like hollyhocks or delphiniums, rising up the curtain. Trailing ivy looks very effective, and a dramatic design could be achieved by stenciling a hanging basket onto the curtain to give a kind of trompe-l'oeil effect.

Traditional curtains can also be decorated with stencils, but because they are usually drawn back, the best design is a border along the edges or a random pattern all over the curtain. Wooden shutters look stunning when decorated with a stencil design, and these make an attractive alternative to curtains.

Materials
- Voile curtains
- Butterfly, bee, or other insect stencils
- Fabric paints or oil-based stenciling crayons in light blue, dark blue, and gold, or colors of your choice
- Size 2 and 4 stenciling brushes
- Glass palette

1

2

1 Begin by washing your curtains so they are clean and preshrunk. Make sure you have suitably sized brushes for each color you will use. The butterfly and bee motifs create a random pattern all over the curtain, so no advance planning is necessary.

3

3 These butterflies are created with a two-part stencil. First, randomly stencil the butterflies all over the fabric with the paler blue color. It is essential to use a lighter color first and then shade with a darker color, because the reverse is not successful.

2 Starting from either the top or bottom of the curtain, depending on your preference, stencil a random collection of bees across the fabric. Here the bees have been stenciled with a bright gold paint for impact.

Helpful Tips
- Other fabrics can be used to produce this beautiful curtain, such as gauze muslin, lightweight muslin lining, netting, or any other semi-transparent fabric that allows the light to shine through.

4 Add the darker blue
shading in the center
of the butterfly. Alternatively,
you could use gold again in
the middle of some
butterflies and the dark blue
for the rest.

5 When the decoration is
complete, read the
manufacturer's instructions
that accompany the fabric
paints and carefully iron the
curtains on both sides to
set the design.

ABOVE A random selection
of insects looks more
impressive than a
regimented pattern for a
delicate curtain, such as this
one. Other small stencils,
such as tiny flowers and
buds, fleur-de-lis, and gold
stars, could look equally
impressive. You may even
want to experiment with a
white-on-white effect, using
white or cream fabric paints
for a very subtle decoration.

OPPOSITE A sprinkling of
blue butterflies and gold
bees lightly decorate this
plain voile curtain. Soft and
metallic colors enhance the
effect natural light makes
when it shines through the
curtain.

Floral Features

Embellishing Plain Curtain Tie-backs

Plain curtain tie-backs can be made at home, if you are handy with a needle and thread, or plain cotton or muslin versions can be purchased and then decorated. Because the tie-backs are wrapped around the curtains to hold them back, you will need to attach plain or decorative cup-hooks into the wall at the appropriate positions so the ties can be secured.

Fabric paints are necessary for this project, because it is convenient to be able to wash the tie-backs. If you would prefer to use other paints, use the oil-based stencil crayons, but remember that the finished tie-backs can not be washed. Whether this is a major problem for you or not depends on how rigorously you carry out your cleaning routine and how much the tie-backs would be used. If the tie-backs are only hanging decoratively in a spare bedroom, and will not be subjected to dust and dirt, you might choose to use the same paints you have used on the walls so the colors match exactly.

Although the design shown here is a fairly simple one, the amount of space to stencil on the tie-back is somewhat limited. Even the broadest tie-backs will need a fairly dainty stencil design that is small and uncomplicated enough to fit comfortably into the space allowed.

If the tie-backs are to be used with heavily stenciled curtains, then just a spray of leaves, a posy of flowers, or a butterfly or two will be sufficient.

You may like to make curtains to match your tie-backs (see pages 92–5), and you can use either the same stencil design on both items or repeat a small detail from the curtain design onto the tie-backs. Another successful combination for home furnishings is to use plain-colored curtains with tie-backs that are decorated with the same design as a stenciled border or random pattern on the walls. Plain curtains in a simple, solid color make a good contrast to stenciled walls and tie-backs.

Curtain pelmets can also be stenciled, whether they are constructed from hardboard or wood and painted with several coats of latex paint, or made from plain fabric, such as cotton or muslin lining. A hardboard pelmet can be cut with a jigsaw along the edge to match the outline of your stencil, and this makes a highly ornamental and unusual feature in the room. Stenciled pelmets and tie-backs look impressive when used with plain curtains, but you may prefer to decorate all elements, depending on the complexity of your design and the effect you want to achieve.

Materials
- Plain cotton or muslin tie-backs
- Floral stencils (see Stencil Templates, page 103)
- Fabric paints in pale green, pink, and brown, or colors of your choice
- Size 2 and 4 stenciling brushes
- Glass palette

1 You will need to have suitably sized brushes for each color you intend to use. Make sure your plain tie-backs are clean, and the stencil either fits the tie-backs perfectly or is flexible enough to have individual leaves added to stretch or widen the design. Paint in the leaves; in this case, a pale green was chosen to match the piping.

2 Add a pale pink to the outer petals on the flowers. You could use a variety of colors if you wish, or just one pale pink and one darker pink for shading and contrast.

3 Add the darker color in the center and on a few of the edges of the flowers to give shading and detail to the design. A darker green could also be used to shade the leaves, if you wished.

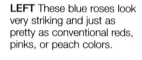

LEFT These blue roses look very striking and just as pretty as conventional reds, pinks, or peach colors.

4 Iron the finished design carefully to set the fabric paints, following the manufacturer's instructions. Do make sure that the paint is dry first, because it is easy to smudge your design if you try to iron it too soon after stenciling.

5 Although it will barely be seen, decorating the back of the tie-back is a nice touch. This will be glimpsed when the curtains are closed and the tie-back hangs down unused. Begin with the leaves.

6 To finish the back of the tie-back, apply the pink paint to the flower, then shade with the brown color. You could also use a simple spray of leaves or a couple of flowers for this detail.

Helpful Tips
● If you have a patterned curtain, copy a motif from the curtains to create a stencil for the tie-backs. Use one single color taken from the colors of the curtain, and you will have plain tie-backs with a stenciled motif that matches your curtain fabric.

OPPOSITE These eye-catching rose tie-backs look beautiful when set against plain curtains. The design gracefully fills the space on the tie-backs, but you could also use just one or two small simple rosebuds.

Index

Stencil Templates

In this section you will find templates for some of the stencils used in this book to get you started on your first projects. Simply follow the instructions for tracing and cutting out a stencil given on pages 12-13, place your newly cut stencil on the wall or object you want to decorate, and apply your paint—what could be easier!